Contents

WITHDRAWN

Introduction

Have you ever watched couponers on TV walk away with carts full of groceries for pennies and wondered just how they did it? Have you ever walked out of the store with your own expensive cart full of groceries and still had nothing in the house to make for dinner? Have you ever struggled to stretch your dollars to buy food, fill up the gas tank, and still pay your bills?

If so, couponing is for you.

It's no stretch to say that couponing has changed my life. Like most of you, I used to spend way too much at the store and have too little to show for it. I used to wonder where all my money went, but then look in my cupboards and find nothing there to cook. I used to worry about how we would feed the family, fill up the tank, and pay the bills—not to mention save for the future!

Then everything changed.

A few years ago, we were in the middle of adopting our second son from South Korea. Our income was down at the same time our expenses were up, and continuing to climb. Not only was international adoption incredibly expensive, we were adding another member to the family—one who would need diapers, formula, and all those other expensive baby items.

I wondered why these things had to be so expensive. As a (former) librarian, my first thought was to go online and start researching how people saved money at the store. I found a wonderful community of people who were eager to share their tips and their trips, took my first tentative steps into the brave new world of couponing, and never looked back.

Instant Savings

The cool thing about couponing is you will start to see savings almost immediately. On my first planned couponing trip to the store, I saved 60 percent off my bill with coupons: I was hooked! Some very simple changes in the way you shop and match up coupons with sales will have a dramatic impact on your bottom line at checkout.

And the savings get better as you go along. When you learn how to use coupons together with sales to stock up on items for pennies on the dollar, you never have to pay full price again. When you shop from your nicely stocked pantry, you continue to save every single week you don't have to pay full price. After you have spent a couple of months building up that stockpile of staples, you'll really start to see the savings pile up.

We All Need to Coupon

In today's less-than-cheery economy, many of us are under new pressures to save. Our incomes are down at the same time prices on everything from food to gas are up. While we have less control over some of our bills, we do have control over what we pay for everyday essentials at the grocery store and drugstore. Take control back from the stores and the manufacturers, and take control of your own finances.

You'll be in good company: couponing today has become much more hip—and most of the myths about who uses coupons were never actually true. Middle-class, college-educated consumers are the most likely to use coupons, and the rise of electronic and printable coupons means that you need to have a computer with Internet access to participate fully.

Popular primetime shows have also gotten many people interested in couponing, and the ongoing economic downturn means that you'll see other people in the checkout lines with their own handfuls of coupons. Get on the bandwagon and find out why you should join them—and come join me in couponing conversation over at MashupMom.com.

What You'll Find Here

This book is divided into four parts:

In **Part 1, Couponing Basics,** begin by looking at your shopping habits and learning how to stock up on sales. Then learn the difference between manufacturer, store, and electronic coupons, and where to find each. Go online to print out more coupons than you'll ever find in your Sunday newspaper, and then take a look at some common couponing myths and facts—including the surprising reality that you can often save more on name-brand products with coupons than you can at warehouse clubs or by buying generic.

Part 2, Using Coupons Effectively, builds on the basics and explains how to coupon effectively to maximize your savings. Learn how being flexible translates into huge savings at the store, and how to shop from and menu plan around your stockpile. Most importantly, you'll find out about the money-back coupons and rewards programs that pay *you* to shop at both grocery stores and drugstores. Lastly, you'll stack all those savings methods together to get items for pennies on the dollar, or even for free.

Couponing isn't just for grocery stores anymore, and in **Part 3, Online and Mobile Couponing,** we start with cash-back programs that pay rebates for online shopping. Daily deals sites save you 50 percent or more on everything from dining to local attractions, and you can also save on dining out by finding online coupons, gift certificates, and codes. Use coupon codes to save a percentage off every online purchase while you comparison shop for the best deals. Learn the surprising ins and outs of shopping Amazon, and get groceries and household items shipped to your door for less than the local store. Add mobile apps and sign up for SMS coupons so that you can coupon on the go.

In **Part 4, Planning and Organizing,** you find out how to acquire more coupons and organize them so that you can plot out your trips to the store. Then delve into the world of online coupon blogs and forums—and use these tools to help you plan out effective shopping trips. Plan and coupon for your priorities, whether those include eating organic, shopping around dietary restrictions, or couponing in rural areas. We'll then talk about how to organize the items you buy and places to donate your bounty. Lastly, a look at the future of couponing and how changing policies and procedures will affect the way you plan.

Extras

TIPS AND TRICKS

Here you'll find tips that you can take shopping with you.

HEADS-UP

Keep these warnings in mind to avoid missing deals and to keep the savings rolling in.

DEFINITIONS

Find out what some of that confusing couponing lingo means.

COUPON QUIPS

Use these bits of expert advice to help you save even more as you master couponing.

Acknowledgments

Just as with couponing, you never write a book in a vacuum. Thanks to all three of my boys for their patience while Mom was preoccupied with writing all summer. My lovely editor, Lori Cates Hand, who saw the potential in this project and convinced me to take it on in the first place. Thanks to her and the other *Complete Idiot's Guide* folks for making sure this got off the ground.

This also wouldn't have been possible without all the readers and commenters at MashupMom.com, who put proof to the idea that many pairs of eyes are better than one. Their feedback, along with the ongoing conversation on many wonderful couponing blogs and forums, creates a couponing community that's stronger for its diversity.

Trademarks

All terms mentioned in this book that are known to be or are suspected of being trademarks or service marks have been appropriately capitalized. Alpha Books and Penguin Group (USA) Inc. cannot attest to the accuracy of this information. Use of a term in this book should not be regarded as affecting the validity of any trademark or service mark.

Couponing Basics

Everyone gets started somewhere! Think of the following chapters as your Coupons 101 intro class. We'll walk step by step through the basics, starting with a good hard look at your current shopping habits. Most of us shop badly—it's true. For instance, we often pick up what we want, when we want, for whatever price it happens to be. Small changes can have a big impact, so learn to plan your shopping trips around sales.

When your prerequisite shopping habits re-do is out of the way, then it's time to talk coupons. Learn about the different types: manufacturer, store, electronic, printable. Learn how to tell the difference and the best places to find each.

We'll wrap it up with a look at common couponing myths and facts, including the biggie: You really *can* save more by combining coupons with sales than you can by going generic or shopping the big box stores. We'll also talk a bit about ethical couponing, and how you can coupon effectively without being unkind or extreme.

Getting Started

In This Chapter

- Change your shopping habits for major savings
- Stock up on items at their lowest price
- Learn when a sale is really a sale
- Combine coupons with sales for maximum savings

In today's economy, more Americans are using coupons than ever before. Since the recession hit in 2008, coupon usage has been rising steadily for the first time since 1992. We redeemed 27 percent more coupons in 2009 than in 2008, and coupon redemption was up another 3 percent in 2010 over 2009. Both coupon distribution and redemption hit record levels in 2010, and Valassis (who puts out the RedPlum coupon inserts in Sunday papers) reports that over 78 percent of consumers have used coupons regularly over the last year.

While more of us use coupons out of necessity, most of us don't really know how to use those coupons effectively. What do I mean by effectively? I mean, using coupons to get many everyday items for pennies on the dollar—and often even for free! That's exactly what you'll learn how to do throughout this book, as we talk about the best ways to get the most bang for your couponing buck.

Let's get started by thinking about your shopping habits, and how making small changes in the way you shop translates into big savings later—even before you ever clip a single coupon.

Take a Look at Your Shopping Habits

I know how most of you shop, because it's exactly the way I used to shop, and it's how I see others shop every time I go to the store. You might make a shopping list of what you're out of and whatever you feel like eating this week. (Or, maybe you don't even do that—you just go to the store and wing it!) You head to the grocery store where you quickly fill your cart, and maybe throw in a few extra eye-catching goodies or last-minute items.

You head to the checkout, where the total on the register climbs ever higher. Maybe you use a couple of coupons, if you remember to dig them out of your purse or clip them out of that same day's newspaper, but they barely make a dent in your overall total.

With these shopping patterns it's very easy to get frustrated and to conclude that couponing isn't worth the effort. Trust me: it is! When I go to the grocery store now, my goal is to save 50 to 90 percent off every grocery bill by using coupons. When I hit the drugstore, I combine coupons with sales and promotions to get most of my toiletries and over-the-counter medications for free. I live in an area of the country where prices are high, and where none of the stores doubles coupons. So if I can do it, you can do it, too!

COUPON QUIPS

Food costs aren't trivial; as of August 2011, the USDA estimates that a moderate budget for the average cost of food at home for a family of four with two small children is $843.60 a month—and that's just for food alone (www.cnpp.usda.gov/USDAFoodCost-Home.htm)! Now, start adding in everyday items like diapers, shampoo, toothpaste, and paper towels, and you can see how these items really add up. If you start slashing your grocery bills with the strategic use of coupons, you're easily looking at hundreds of dollars a month in savings.

While we don't have a lot of control over the cost of many items in our family's budget, food items and health and beauty aisle (HBA) items are areas in which you can reap significant savings fairly quickly.

In order to really save at the store though, you need to take a good hard look at your shopping habits and work to develop some new ones. If you follow these simple steps, you'll start to see a dramatic reduction in your grocery bill in just a few short weeks.

Stock Up During Sales

When you go to the store, you'll notice that prices are all over the place. A box of cereal that is on super-saver special for $1.49 this week might jump up to $3.95 the next week, then bop down to $2.50 the week after, with no apparent rhyme or reason. Stores often run their lowest priced items as loss leaders to get you in the door, knowing that you'll probably do the rest of your shopping at their everyday high prices.

Stores also know that most people tend to grab one or two of the loss leaders at that great price, and then will be in again to buy another one of that very same item a week or two later. As a small exercise, pretend you're buying something more expensive, like stocks. Just like in the stock market, you want to buy low, and you want to think long term.

Instead of grabbing just one box of cheap cereal when it's at $1.49, think "Hmm. My kids really like this cereal, and they easily go through a box a week. How many boxes are they going to chow down on before it goes for $1.49 again?"

Products tend to hit their lowest price point about once every 12 weeks. This isn't a hard-and-fast rule, but it's a good guideline for getting started and thinking about how many items to stock up on at any given time. So let's say cereal's priced really low this week. Your family eats a lot of it and you're down to your last box. Instead of grabbing just a box or two at that great price, maybe you grab 8 boxes, or maybe you even pick up 10 boxes! (We talk later about using coupons to bring that price down even further, too.)

If you buy all that extra cereal this week when it's priced at $1.49, you can just keep "shopping" from your pantry until it goes on sale again. Next week, your kids (or husband, or you) will likely have gone through a whole box of cereal. If that very same box of cereal is now up to $3.95 at the store, you don't need to run out and buy another one. Grab a new box off your own shelf, and you've just saved $2.46. (You, of course, want not to over-buy on items that your family might get tired of, but this is a good strategy for tried-and-true products and those with long expiration dates that you can take a break from and then pull out as "new" again later.)

The next week, maybe that same cereal goes on "sale" for $2.50—but you don't have to buy any, because you already bought it at $1.49 two weeks ago. You are saving a buck or two every single week you shop from your pantry, until your cereal again hits its rock-bottom price and you stock up again.

Think about the long-term impact this type of shopping can have on your family's budget, not only with cereal, but with many other commonly used items. When you shop low for cereal, for peanut butter, and for toothpaste, you can keep working off your stockpile until those items hit their lowest price points again. How much would you save each week if you never paid full price for dozens of commonly used items?

> **COUPON QUIPS**
>
> Stores try to get you in the door by selling a loss leader at a rock-bottom price, often taking a loss on that one item in order to lure in shoppers who will also buy more expensive items once in the door. Buy loss leaders and add them to your stockpile of items you purchase for very cheap—or for free—and then shop from your own shelves until you're able to get another deal. Your stockpile will grow to include a supply of many of your family's commonly used items, allowing you to save every single week you don't buy those items for full price.

You've probably heard that phrase "buy low, sell high" in terms of the stock market. Well if you "buy low" at the grocery store or drugstore, you have the potential to save a bigger percentage than most of us are making on any of our investments right now!

When building your stockpile, don't worry about becoming one of those over-the-top hoarders you see on TV; there's a huge difference between stockpiling and hoarding items.

When you stockpile, you purchase a supply for your family to use and keep it to a reasonable number of items your family will consume before their expiration dates. You don't let it take over your house, and you don't let it take over your life. When you hoard, you buy items you don't need just for the sheer thrill of buying and having, collect hundreds of items your family will never use, and get upset at the thought of actually using the unnecessary items you purchase.

> **COUPON QUIPS**
>
> Few people comment about customers buying an item in bulk at a warehouse store. Leaving Costco, Sam's Club, or BJ's with a carload of economy-size items is seen as both thrifty and smart. When you stockpile it's like you're buying in bulk, but instead of buying a single economy-size jar of peanut butter (that will go bad before you get to the bottom) you buy several smaller jars of peanut butter that stay fresh on your shelf until you need to shop from your pantry.

When you buy individual items in quantity, you are able to maximize your savings.

Know When a Deal Is Really a Deal

Stores and manufacturers are not necessarily on your side. They want to sell products and make money; you want to buy products and save money. Manufacturers and stores spend a lot of time, money, and effort getting us to shop a certain way. A smart shopper knows that just because an item is displayed attractively or advertised heavily, it doesn't necessarily mean it's a good deal for you. Here are some things you want to watch out for.

First, watch for in-store coupons. These are great—of course we like coupons!—but manufacturers place coupons in stores to help fuel impulse buys. You might not have planned to purchase an item, but may decide to add it to your cart anyway if there is a handy coupon right in front of it. Don't fall into this trap: happily accept the coupons they so kindly provide, but use them wherever and whenever you are able to score the best deal.

Don't be fooled by pretty displays or advertising. Only some of the items listed in your weekly grocery store circulars, for example, are actually on sale. Stores often put their best sales on the front and back pages of their flier in order to bring people in, but many of the "sales" listed on the inside pages are really just advertising items they want to move this week or items that manufacturers want to promote.

Just because a store emblazons a big yellow SALE logo over a product, doesn't mean it's actually a good price. Sure, a $7.99 item that's selling for $7.98 this week is technically on sale, but that doesn't really help anyone save.

Stores try to move regular-price items with their in-store displays and endcaps (displays at the ends of aisles), as well. One clever tactic? Displaying commonly used products together to encourage impulse buys. An endcap display, for instance, might contain hamburger and hot dog buns, mustard and ketchup, and chips and marinades. Maybe just one item in the whole shebang is on sale, but the display reminds you that you need these products for your upcoming backyard barbecue, so you throw several in your cart—even if different brands on the regular shelf might actually be on sale or be a better deal.

After you coupon for a bit, you'll start getting a sense of good sale prices for the items you often buy. People used to keep a price book for this purpose, writing down the prices of their favorite items every week as they fluctuated in order to get a sense of the patterns. There are less time-consuming ways now to see if a deal is really a deal, which we'll talk about in Chapter 15.

TIPS AND TRICKS

If you do want to keep your own price book, you can find a template online to help get you started. Use whatever tool works for you—a spiral notebook and a pen, an Excel spreadsheet, or a Word template. Just use a blank page for each product and record the following basic information for the products you want to track every time you go to the store:

- Store name
- Brand
- Size
- Unit Cost
- Date

Over time you'll start to see the pricing patterns for your favorite products.

Your second rule of thumb is this: always pay attention to the fine print. For example, one of my local grocery stores is notorious for putting 12-packs of Coke and Pepsi products on a buy-two-get-two free sale. They emblazon *buy two, get two free* on huge signs in store, create multiple free standing or endcap displays, and list it in large lettering in their weekly ad.

What does the fine print say? "Save up to $11.98 on four." This means that those 12-packs of soda are actually on sale for $5.99 each (yikes!), which makes them four for $11.98, or about $3 apiece on a buy-two-get-two free sale.

This is an okay, but not fantastic, sale price for name-brand soda; but I'll always see people loading up their carts convinced they are getting something free. Those same shoppers wouldn't buy in the same quantities if the soda were simply listed as 4 for $12 (4/$12)— and on this sale, you actually have to buy four to get the reduced price, even if you really only wanted one 12-pack.

In this soda example, you would have to buy in quantity to get the savings. But sometimes stores deliberately word their sales fliers to make you think you have to buy large numbers of an item, even if you'll get the same savings when just buying one or two.

For instance, you often see stores advertising a "10 for $10" sale. Unless the fine print says something like "when you buy 10" or "must buy 10," this just means that every item in that sale costs $1. You can buy 1, 5, or 25, and each will simply cost $1. Again, look at the fine print.

Now, Add Coupons

You'll find more specific strategies later on in this book to help you maximize your coupon savings. Keep in mind, though, when you start thinking about changing the way that you shop and how to avoid being taken in by deals that aren't really deals, you see that adding coupons on top of sales can really take you far.

Think back to that rock-bottom–priced box of cereal, for example. Let's say that you're buying 10 boxes of cereal this week at $1.49

each, because your kids go through a box of cereal each week and you want to stock up on enough to last until it hits that lowest price point again. What happens when you add coupons on top of that sale-price savings?

---

10 sale-priced cereal boxes = $14.90

5 coupons for $1 off 2 boxes = -$5.00

$14.90
-$5.00
‾‾‾‾‾‾
  $9.90

By using coupons, you're paying under $1.00 for each box of cereal—and you'll see an even bigger savings when that cereal goes back up to $3.95 and you can just shop from your pantry next week!

When you add a coupon to an everyday high price at your grocery store, it's hard to see real savings. Using coupons together with sale prices enables you to see extreme savings at the grocery store. In our cereal example, stacking a coupon with a sale price (using two types of savings on one item) results in a savings of 75 percent off the everyday price of that cereal. Now imagine getting that same 75 percent savings on most of the everyday food and HBA items you buy. That can have a serious impact on your household budget.

TIPS AND TRICKS

Using coupons with sales gives you a bigger percentage of savings. At its everyday $3.95 price, a $1 off 2 ($1/2) coupon for your boxes of cereal is a drop in the bucket. You're still paying $3.45 for each, a mere 12.5 percent savings. At your cereal's rock-bottom sale price of $1.49 though, you're saving 62 percent off its normal price on the store sale alone. That very same $1 off 2 coupon gives you an additional 33 percent savings off the sale price, and a 75 percent savings off the everyday price—which over time makes a much bigger difference to your household budget.

Your biggest key to maximizing your savings with coupons is to wait for a sale to match up with your coupons. When you watch those dramatic staged-for-television shopping trips with cartfuls of items and hundreds of coupons, the couponers pictured on TV aren't just walking into the store and buying products willy-nilly: they're waiting for rock-bottom prices to combine with their high-value coupons.

You don't have to copy this "biggest trip ever" behavior and fill up nine carts with cereal to realize similarly high percentages of savings. The principle holds true whether you're buying 5 boxes of cereal or 200 boxes of cereal: wait for the rock-bottom sale price and stack coupons with sales for maximum savings. When it comes to couponing, patience really is a virtue.

The Least You Need to Know

- Maximize savings by changing how you shop: shop sales and stockpile common items to avoid ever having to pay full price.
- Stores and manufacturers spend a lot of energy marketing particular products to us. We don't have to buy!
- Over time, you'll get to know whether a "deal" is really a deal or not.
- Always combine coupons with sale prices at the store to get the best possible deals.

Manufacturer, Store, and Electronic Coupons

In This Chapter

- Manufacturer coupons act as a form of payment
- Store coupons act as a store discount
- Load electronic coupons for automatic savings

When learning how to use coupons effectively, it's important to understand the different types of coupons and how each can be used. This makes more sense when you start thinking about where exactly your coupon savings are coming from with each type.

Technology is also changing couponing as manufacturers move to clipless methods of coupon delivery. Companies enjoy the control of electronic coupons, which enables them to put stricter limits on the number of coupons that can be used by any one person and to track consumers' purchasing habits. Consumers' advantage lies in electronic coupons' ease of use—nothing to clip, and nothing to remember to bring to the store, other than your loyalty card.

This chapter explains everything you need to know about manufacturer coupons, store coupons, and electronic coupons, from where to find them to when and where you can use each.

Manufacturer Coupons

Manufacturer coupons are released by the company that makes a particular product, and most coupons in your Sunday newspaper inserts are manufacturer coupons. These generally say "manufacturer coupon" at the top and have a redemption address and instructions to retailers on where to send in for reimbursement.

That last part is the most important to couponers. Your local store is reimbursed by the manufacturer for each of these coupons, plus a small handling fee. This means that manufacturer coupons work like a form of payment for the products. When you hand your cashier a $1 coupon for a product you are buying, it's almost like you're handing her a $1 bill—because in the end, the store gets that $1 (plus a small handling fee for its trouble).

Manufacturer coupons can be used at any store, although some stores have rules restricting the types of coupons they accept. This is wonderful news for couponers, because you can use any manufacturer coupon at whichever store has the best sale. Pull a manufacturer coupon off the shelf at one local grocery store, put it in your pocket, and bring it to another store where that item is on sale—or save your coupon for a future sale.

So where do you find these manufacturer coupons?

In the Newspaper

First, check your Sunday (or, in some papers, Friday) newspaper inserts. This is still the most common method of coupon distribution, and you'll want to be sure to pick up at least one Sunday newspaper each week. Also, be sure to pick up the largest circulation newspaper available in your local area. Since manufacturers want to get the most bang for their coupon buck, they'll put the most and the highest value coupons in the biggest local paper.

In the Store

Some stores include manufacturer coupons right in their weekly ads. Use these just as you would coupons from the Sunday inserts.

You'll also find manufacturer coupons next to item displays in stores to boost sales by fueling impulse buys. You'll find coupons everywhere, from tables offering samples, to *blinkie* machines on the shelves, to *peelies* and *hangtags* right on the products themselves.

DEFINITION

Couponers have developed their own lingo for coupons you find at the store. **Peelies** are stuck right onto a product—you peel the coupon sticker off and use it. It's considered impolite to take a peelie off a product you're not purchasing at that time, because this leaves a sticky residue to show others they're missing a discount. **Hangtags** are coupons in separate tags that hang right around an item's neck. Lastly, **blinkies** refer to the coupons that come out of machines with little blinking lights attached to shelves at many stores. Some stores have replaced blinkies with pull-out dispensers that lack the lights, but the term persists.

You might also find brochures or small booklets containing multiple coupons from different manufacturers, and these are often higher value than those found in the newspaper inserts. Take a brisk walk up and down the aisles (consider it your exercise for the day!) and see what you can spot the next time you're shopping at your local grocery store.

Online

It's becoming more and more common for companies to distribute some (or all) of their coupons on the Internet. This is a great way to get more coupons than are available in your local paper. We discuss online printable coupons in depth in Chapter 3.

When you sign up online for mailing lists and product promotions, companies often include coupons in the mailers they send. Always check your junk mail to see if it includes any coupons you can use at the store.

All Around

I've found wonderful manufacturer coupons everywhere from pediatricians' and dentists' offices to festivals and open houses.

Many magazines, especially "women's interest magazines," contain pull-out coupon inserts or have coupons printed directly in some of their ads. These are often higher value coupons than in the newspaper, or promote a special holiday or other sales.

TIPS AND TRICKS

Take advantage of free magazine subscription offers to help up your stock of coupons. Sites to check for free subscriptions include freebizmag.com, www.valuemags.com, and rewardsgold.com.

See a coupon? Take one and put it in your pocket, because you never know when it might come in handy later.

Store Coupons

Store coupons are issued by an individual store and are deducted at the register as a store discount. Stores issue a coupon for a product as an alternative way to put the item on sale, but you need to use the coupon in order to get that sale price. Store coupons do not act as a form of payment for products in the same way manufacturer coupons do.

Store coupons can make for some great deals since stores often use coupon items as loss leaders to bring in traffic.

Store coupons are redeemable only at the store that issued the coupon, although some stores in select parts of the country do accept local competitors' store coupons. (We'll talk more in Chapter 16 about getting to know your local stores' policies; local competitors are defined in various ways, and only a few stores do this.)

When you go to use a store coupon, read the wording carefully to see if it has any additional requirements. Some, for example, require an additional $10 purchase—meaning that you need to add another $10 worth of merchandise to your cart in addition to the product(s) you want to purchase with the coupon. Others have limits, such as one per customer, or one per transaction or shopping trip. Knowing the limits and restrictions on your store coupon before you go will save you grief at the register.

Where do you find store coupons?

In the Newspaper and in the Mail

Occasionally, major chains like Target or Walgreens include store coupons in the coupon inserts found in your Sunday newspaper. These are often regional, meaning that some parts of the country receive either a separate store insert or ad pages inside the regular inserts containing these coupons, while other regions do not.

Also check the ads for local stores in your Sunday paper, your mid-week paper, or in the mail. These often contain store coupons that you can clip before your trip.

In the Store

When you walk in a store, look for brochures, pamphlets, and stacks of coupons up front. Walgreens releases monthly brochures full of store coupons that are found up front near the weekly ads, as well as additional little thematic brochures that are occasionally found throughout the store. Other stores release occasional brochures containing store coupons, which you'll find on stands inside the store. Sometimes you'll also find a few store coupons mixed in with the manufacturer coupons in larger in-store multi-coupon brochures and booklets.

Online

Visit store websites (such as www.Target.com and www. meijermealbox.com/) and look for a coupons or specials link. Some stores provide only printable store coupons on their site; others contain both store and manufacturer printable coupons.

HEADS-UP

Know before you go how coupons work with sales tax in your state. Since store coupons come off as a store discount, they reduce the selling price of an item—which also reduces your taxable total. If you have a $2 store coupon for a $5 item, you'll pay tax only on the post-store-coupon $3 price.

When it comes to manufacturer coupons though, some states tax the entire pre-manufacturer-coupon price of each item. In others, manufacturer coupons reduce your taxable total, just as store coupons do. After a shopping trip or two, you'll learn how your state does things, but on high-tax items, this can make a significant difference in your bottom line. An item that's free with coupons is not really free if you're paying 8.5 percent or more in tax on your precoupon total.

Knowing the Difference

Sometimes it can be difficult to tell whether a coupon is a store or a manufacturer coupon. Clues include the following:

- Store coupons have "Store coupon" or "[*name of store*] coupon" (such as "Target coupon" or "Safeway coupon") at the top.

- Store coupons generally do not have numbers under their barcodes, or numbers start with a bunch of zeros.

- Manufacturer coupons generally say "Manufacturer coupon" at the top, or sometimes say "Retailer coupon."

- Manufacturer coupons always have a redemption address.

- Manufacturer coupons with old-style barcodes (not the new GS1 barcodes that the industry is moving towards) have barcode numbers that start with either a 5 or a 9.

We'll talk more in Chapter 8 about why it's important to know the differences between types of coupons, but for now, it's just important to know where you can use each.

At some stores, your cashier will take the store coupons you use and keep them in her register in a separate stack from the manufacturer coupons. At others, such as Walgreens, they don't even need to keep the coupon—they just scan it from the ad and the register tracks the discounts and which store coupons were used. You'll get to know the policies and practices of your usual stores.

Confusingly, some manufacturer coupons may display a single store's logo or contain verbiage such as "Redeemable at Dollar General" or "Available at Walmart." Unless the coupon says it's redeemable *only* at a certain store, you can use it at any store that accepts manufacturer coupons. (And some stores will even accept all manufacturer coupons, regardless of this wording!) This is one place where it's useful to know that manufacturer coupons work as a form of payment for your item. Even if another store's logo is printed on a manufacturer coupon, your store will still be reimbursed by the manufacturer.

Some cashiers may get confused by wording or a logo that suggests a manufacturer coupon must be redeemed at a particular store. As long as there isn't a store policy against taking these coupons, remain pleasant, point out the wording that shows it's a manufacturer coupon, and ask "Why don't we see if it scans?"

TIPS AND TRICKS

A special note about Walgreens: although coupons found in their monthly in-store booklets on the ad racks are store coupons, they say "manufacturer coupon" in the wording. This can be confusing to customers and cashiers, but trust me, they are store coupons. They don't have a redemption address and they don't have a full barcode. Your cashier can just scan them right out of the booklet rather than tearing out and keeping the coupon, since they come off as a store discount at the register.

Electronic Coupons

Many stores, especially larger national chains, now participate in electronic coupon (e-coupon) programs. There are many of these, but basically they all work the same way: you load electronic coupons right onto your grocery store's loyalty card from a list of available coupons, and they come off as an automatic discount at the register when you buy qualifying products.

Your local grocery stores may participate in one or more e-coupon programs. You can either visit the various e-coupon sites to see which stores participate, or visit each of your local stores' websites to see what programs they participate in. Stores that don't use a loyalty card don't generally participate in e-coupon programs, since you need a card to load these coupons.

Manufacturers really like e-coupons since they allow stricter control over how many coupons each customer can use. Let's say a company releases 1,000 coupons for its product; it can make sure that 1,000 consumers each have access to one of the 1,000 manufacturer coupons (thus creating 1,000 potential repeat customers) instead of 100 consumers each using 10 of the coupons.

Manufacturers are looking for the broadest possible market for their products, the idea being that customers who purchase a product because of a coupon may turn into repeat buyers if they like the item. E-coupons enable manufacturers to limit coupon usage and to thwart high-volume shoppers who go out of their way to get large quantities of identical paper coupons.

HEADS-UP

Electronic coupons can be frustrating when things go wrong—and they sometimes do! When an e-coupon fails to come off at the register, you don't have a piece of paper to point to as you do when using paper coupons. Cashiers generally can't tell what's loaded onto your card, although some stores now have laptops where customers can log in and present proof. Pay attention to your receipt and be sure e-coupons have triggered before you leave the store; be prepared to argue your case or return items if you wouldn't have purchased them without that anticipated e-coupon discount.

While there are multiple electronic coupon sites, each works pretty much the same way. What e-coupon programs might your local stores participate in? Here are a few examples of some of the largest.

Cellfire

Cellfire (www.cellfire.com) requires you to enter your mobile phone number to register, which serves as your login ID—but you don't need to agree to receive texts to participate in the program. When you sign up, you'll also need to give Cellfire the barcode numbers off the back of your grocery card(s), which then allows you to load electronic coupons onto those cards from its site.

Cellfire partners with a number of grocery chains, including Kroger, Shoprite, Giant Eagle, and Shop n' Save. (As of now, it also partners with some Safeway affiliates in certain states; however Safeway is in the process of disengaging its business from Cellfire as it gradually rolls out its own Just for U e-coupon program across the country.)

Cellfire adds a new set of e-coupons every two weeks, and you generally have a month to use each batch before they expire. After an e-coupon expires or is used, it simply disappears off your card and is no longer available. You need to go back to the Cellfire site to load each new batch of coupons onto your card before you can use them (and, you need to add each e-coupon of interest individually). However if you create an account on their site, they'll email you a reminder when new e-coupons become available, and again as they're about to expire.

Each e-coupon comes off at the register only once. For instance, say you have an e-coupon on your card for $.75/2 Nature Valley granola bars. If you buy two boxes, the $.75 e-coupon will automatically come off at the register. If, however, you buy four boxes, you still get only one $.75 discount, even if you buy them over multiple shopping trips.

Shortcuts

The next major electronic coupon site, Shortcuts (shortcuts.com), partners with a number of the same stores as Cellfire, including Kroger, Shop n' Save, and Giant Eagle. You can register up to two different store cards on the Shortcuts site. To maximize your savings, be sure to load e-coupons on both of these sites if your local store participates in both. Click "FIND A STORE" on the left side of the Shortcuts site to see what chains participate.

> **HEADS-UP**
>
> When you start loading e-coupons from multiple sites, realize that your card can only hold a limited number. You can load a maximum of 75 Shortcuts coupons, for example, and if you load e-coupons from one site and then go to load e-coupons from another, you might find that your card has hit its global limit. It's useful to load e-coupons only for the specific products you are interested in buying. Unfortunately, most sites do not allow you to remove an e-coupon from your card once you have loaded it; you have to either redeem it at the store or wait for it to expire before it disappears off of your account.

Shortcuts works pretty much the same way as Cellfire; you'll have to add each e-coupon of interest onto your card before it will come off at the register. Sign up for their emails to receive alerts when they post a new list of available coupons.

Zavers

If you shop in a different area of the country, check out Zavers (zavers.com), who partners with A&P, Superfresh, Pathmark, Harris Teeter, and more. Zavers allows you to save up to 99 e-coupons per card, which you (again) select from a list of available coupons. Unlike Shortcuts and Cellfire, Zavers does allow you to delete unwanted e-coupons from your account.

Common Questions

You're probably wondering: what will happen if I load the same e-coupon twice? This does happen, either because an electronic coupon for an identical product is available on more than one site (for example, one is on Shortcuts, one is on Cellfire) or because new coupons for some overlapping products are available before the old ones expire.

The short answer is no one really knows before you get to the register! Although coupon sites' FAQs (frequently asked questions) generally say you'll receive the higher-valued e-coupon, both will often come off the same item. Don't count on this always happening, but it can be a nice bonus.

Now what happens when your household has multiple loyalty cards? Let's say you and your significant other each had a card to your local grocery store before you got married, or you've lost cards and registered for new ones over the years. You might think this will allow you to load multiple e-coupons for the items you like, as long as you switch between cards on different shopping trips.

This sometimes does work, allowing you to receive identical e-coupon discounts across multiple cards. Stores, however, don't care for this because it circumvents the limits stores and manufacturers are trying to put on coupon use with electronic coupons. So some stores have begun to automatically link accounts that use the same phone number or mailing address. In this case, when you receive an e-coupon discount off one card, it also disappears off the other linked household card. Just be aware of how this works and realize that you won't generally receive a second discount if you use a second linked card.

Store E-Coupon Programs

Some grocery stores choose to offer their own electronic coupon programs rather than partner with one of the national sites. In this case, their e-coupons are available only for that specific store. As with the major national sites, you'll usually need to create an account on the store's e-coupon site and register your loyalty card number.

Following are a couple of examples of store-specific e-coupon sites. Other stores have their own e-coupon programs, and these are likely to become more prevalent as technology catches up and these programs become more popular with consumers.

Safeway

Safeway-owned stores have one of the biggest store-specific e-coupon sites, Just for U, which Safeway is in the process of rolling out nationwide. (Parts of the country that have not yet moved to Just for U participate in Cellfire and Shortcuts.) As with the major e-coupon sites, you log in to the store's website, see a list of available e-coupons, and load them to your card before you see the savings at the register.

SuperValu

At SuperValu-owned stores, their Avenu e-coupon program can be found at sites like Jewel-Osco's www.saveatjewel.com and Albertsons www.saveatalbertsons.com. If you shop at a SuperValu-owned chain, plug "www.saveat[*name of your local store*].com" into your web browser and check out their e-coupons.

The nice thing about Avenu is that you don't have to create an account or individually load e-coupons. You simply put in the bar-code number from your loyalty card to view the e-coupons that are available today, and once you have viewed the page they are automatically loaded onto your card. E-coupons on Avenu change about once a week, so just pop in weekly to see what's new.

The Least You Need to Know

- Manufacturer coupons work like a form of payment for a product—and can be found all around you!
- Store coupons are another way for a store to provide you with a sale price and can make for great deals.
- Local stores with loyalty cards often participate in one or more e-coupon programs. Load these for savings at the register.

Online Printable Coupons

In This Chapter

- Saving more with printable coupons
- Where to find the most coupons
- Going straight to the manufacturer
- Taking advantage of Facebook and Twitter coupons

If you're not printing coupons online, you're missing out on big savings. Many companies are moving their best coupons out of the Sunday newspaper inserts and onto the Internet, and the only place you'll find coupons for many products is online. A computer, a printer, and basic Internet access is all you need to take advantage of the types of coupons in this chapter.

Before you can print coupons online, you need to learn where to find them. This chapter gives you a road map of the best coupons and shows how to avoid headaches when printing them. Get ready to surf your way to savings!

Why Printables?

Companies often release more or higher-value coupons online than they do anywhere else. They know fewer people subscribe to the Sunday paper than in the past, and many of those who do toss the inserts or use only a few coupons out of them. But consumers who print coupons online are much more likely to be interested in the product and actually use the coupon.

For example, I recently printed an online coupon for $1 off one can of Campbell's Select Harvest soup. The Campbell's coupon in that week's insert was for $1 off *three* cans of Campbell's Select Harvest soup. That's right: the online coupon was three times better than the coupon for the very same product found in the Sunday inserts. Simply by looking online rather than in the paper, I saved more with a higher-value coupon—and I ended up with free soup when it went on sale for $1 a can at my local grocery store.

Even accounting for the cost of your own paper and ink, you can see the potential savings with online coupons are significant. It's worth looking online for coupons to match up with sales and your shopping trips at local stores.

TIPS AND TRICKS

Use online coupon databases like the one at Hot Coupon World (hotcouponworld.com/forums/coupon.php) to find printable coupons for various products. Simply type in the product you're looking for and select "Printable" from the drop-down menu under "Source."

You can also often find coupons online that never make it into the Sunday inserts. Smaller or organic companies, for instance, often can't afford to release a coupon in the newspaper, or may want to specifically target a particular group of consumers. While they might also offer paper coupons in specific stores or in brochures like the monthly *Mambo Sprouts* found at Whole Foods and health food stores, they are moving many of their coupon efforts online.

Saving on Paper and Ink

One of the reasons companies offer higher-value coupons online is that you are using your own paper and ink to print them. Being the coupon-savvy bargain hunter that you are, though, you're going to want to save here as well. So here are a few coupon-printing tips and tricks to conserve your paper, ink, and time.

1. Print coupons in grayscale rather than in color. Why waste your expensive color ink on coupons? Black and white coupons scan just fine at the store.

2. Set your default print settings to "economode," "economy," or "draft" mode. Look in your printer properties, and you'll see a box to check. This conserves ink or toner. If you have an older or very cheap printer, this setting may sometimes result in distorted barcodes, although this should be less of a problem with newer models. If you have trouble scanning coupons at the store, switch back to the regular print setting.

3. Print on scratch paper. Use the backs of junk mail, school papers, or old printouts to print your coupons. After all, when you clip a coupon out of a magazine or newspaper, it has something on the back.

4. When you print from major sites like Coupons.com or SmartSource.com (see later in this chapter for more info on these sites), coupons most often print out three to a page. When selecting coupons to print, always try to print in groups or multiples of three to conserve paper.

5. Use coupons, rewards programs, and rebate offers at office supply stores to stock up on paper and toner at rock-bottom prices (more on these programs later).

6. Shop back-to-school sales for savings on paper, ink, and other office supplies; stock up for the whole year.

Coupon-Printing Software

Each major coupon-printing site requires you to download software, called a coupon printer, onto your computer. This software keeps track of the coupons you print and limits the number of times (usually two) you can print a given coupon from any one computer. Again, this offers manufacturers more control over their coupons and helps them distribute them to a wider number of people. Don't worry: this software is safe and won't harm or slow down your computer.

Another thing the coupon-printing software generally does is assign each coupon an individual dot-scan barcode (the squiggly one in the upper right of the printed coupon) or PIN number, as well as record information about where it was printed. Even if you print two of the same coupon, each will have a unique identifier.

0629 8025 9314 0602

Unique identifiers on printable coupons prevent copying.

This is one big reason to never, ever photocopy Internet-printed coupons. Companies set print limits for a reason, and photocopied coupons won't have these unique identifiers. If manufacturers suspect coupon fraud, copied coupons can be traced back to their source. Just don't do it!

Major Coupon-Printing Sites

There are several major coupon-printing sites, and each contains a different mix of coupons. Where should you start to look for printable coupons? The following table shows some of the major coupon sites you should check out.

Major Coupon-Printing Sites

Site	URL	Advantages
Coupons.com	www.coupons.com	contains the most coupons
SmartSource	smartsource.com	contains unique coupons
RedPlum	www.redplum.com	extras of insert coupons
Coupon Network	www.couponnetwork.com	some higher-value coupons

Most of these sites add and delete coupons throughout the month but do their biggest reset and reload of printable coupons at the first of every month. So try to remember to head back at the beginning of the month to see what's new on each.

What's the hurry? Coupons are available on these sites only until they've hit a set number of total prints, which is determined by the manufacturer. Once coupons have been printed that predetermined number of times, they disappear from the site. A hot, or high-value, printable coupon often hits that print limit within the first day or two of its appearance on the site, and sometimes within a matter of hours. So with printables, you snooze, you really do lose!

HEADS-UP

You can sign up on each of these sites for e-mail alerts or RSS feeds that push alerts of new printable coupons to your e-mail box or RSS reader. Sometimes, however, these e-mails are delayed and when a hot printable coupon can disappear in a matter of hours, it's important to get in early. We'll talk in Chapter 15 about ways to keep updated on hot printable coupons and other time-sensitive topics.

Coupons.com

The first site you'll want to check out is Coupons.com, which is the biggest coupon-printing site around. (If you have seen the TV commercials for "Coupon Suzy," she just redirects you right back over to Coupons.com.) On any given day, Coupons.com usually contains over 100 manufacturer coupons that you can print and bring into your local store to redeem. Just check the ones you want to "clip," then click "print coupons" to print all of your selections at once.

On Coupons.com, you can also sort coupons by category if you're looking for a particular type of item. Look over on the left side and click "Household," for instance, if you're looking for coupons for cleaning products, or click "Pet Care" if you're looking for coupons for dog food.

You'll notice that the site also asks you to enter your ZIP code "for additional savings." The real reason it asks for your ZIP code is that manufacturers like to target coupons toward particular areas of the country where items are selling more or less well. Sometimes the coupon dollar values vary, because areas that double coupons under $1 might get a $1/2 coupon, for instance, rather than $.75/1—but sometimes the actual product mix you see varies as well.

On the Internet, no one knows where you live. What happens if you decide to put in a different ZIP code? You guessed it: You see a different mix of coupons! Since these are generally manufacturer coupons redeemable in any store, you can print out a coupon you see under a California ZIP code and redeem it just fine in a Missouri store. It's as if you were on vacation in California, bought a paper, clipped its coupons, and brought them back home to use in your local store. (Be sure to only print coupons for products that are available in your local stores!)

Believe it or not, I tend to find the most coupons under ZIP code 90210. Maybe the folks in Beverly Hills don't need as many coupons so there are more left for the rest of us. Who knows—but give it a try!

> **HEADS-UP**
>
> Manufacturer coupons are currently transitioning to a new GS1 barcode format. Many manufacturer coupons now contain two barcodes at the bottom, the bottom left in the older format and one to the right of it in the new GS1 format that is machine-readable only. This new barcode can contain much more information, including geographic location. It's possible that, at some point, manufacturer coupons that are released in one region of the country may beep at the register when used at a store in another part of the country. This is not yet a reality, but it will be interesting to see how things play out.

SmartSource.com

Another major coupon-printing site you'll want to visit is SmartSource.com. SmartSource.com is run by News America Marketing, the same company that supplies the SmartSource coupon inserts in your Sunday paper. You'll find some familiar-looking coupons on their site, but also a bunch of printables that never make it to the Sunday inserts.

SmartSource uses a different coupon printer program than Coupons.com, so even if you have already installed the Coupons.com software, you'll also need to download SmartSource's software before you can print from their site.

One important note about SmartSource coupons is that their Java-based coupon-printing software is very slow; it takes coupons much longer to spool up and print than the Coupons.com ones do. Don't get impatient and click off the page, just give your computer some time to think about it.

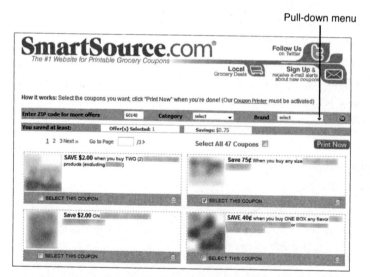

SmartSource.com has a handy pull-down menu of brands.

One useful feature of SmartSource.com is its alphabetical pull-down menu of brands, which allows you to quickly see if they have a specific coupon you're looking for. As with Coupons.com, coupon prints are generally limited to two, you'll find the most new coupons toward the beginning of the month, and you'll find a different mix of coupons under different ZIP codes.

RedPlum

Not to be outdone, the other major newspaper insert, RedPlum, also has its own coupon site at www.RedPlum.com. RedPlum contains many of the same coupons found in that week's insert, allowing you to print another set, but sometimes also offers some unique coupon options. It generally lists fewer coupons than Coupons.com or SmartSource.com, and their coupons tend to hit their print limit much more quickly. (They often release new coupons on Sunday mornings, and the hot coupons will hit their print limit and disappear off the site by late morning or early afternoon.)

Coupon Network

The newest major contender in the printable coupon landscape is Coupon Network, at www.couponnetwork.com. As with the other sites, you'll have to install Coupon Network–specific software on your computer.

One interesting feature of Coupon Network is that, in addition to printable coupons, they feature information about money-back offers at local grocery and drugstores. (We cover those more in Chapter 6.)

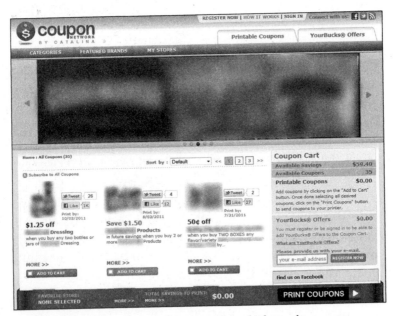

Coupon Network often features unique, higher-value coupons.

Coupon Network also powers the printable coupons on Target's website, which we'll talk about later in this chapter. So if you print a manufacturer coupon on Coupon Network, you won't be able to print another copy at Target; the coupon printer tracks your prints across both sites.

> **TIPS AND TRICKS**
>
> Many smaller and store- or manufacturer-specific coupon-printing sites are actually powered by one or another of the major sites. Mambo Sprouts (www.mambosprouts.com), for example, is powered by Coupons.com—but is specifically dedicated to coupons for natural, organic, and gluten-free products. (See more on couponing for special diets in Part 4.) This is good news for couponers, since once you've installed the coupon printers for each of the four major sites you won't have to install new ones for every site where you want to print another coupon.

Manufacturer Website Coupons

In addition to the hundreds of coupons found on the major coupon-printing sites, you'll also want to check the websites of major manufacturers—or at least the companies that make your family's favorite products. Many companies offer printable coupons on their own sites and many also maintain an e-mail list or newsletter you can subscribe to so you can stay informed about potential future coupon offers.

If you're fond of crescent rolls and fruit snacks, for instance, you might check out Betty Crocker's website; if you're a fan of organic yogurt, sign up over at www.stonyfield.com. Check your pantry to see who manufactures your favorite products, then visit their sites to see what you can find.

As with major coupon-printing sites, many manufacturers reset their coupons (or offer a new batch) at the beginning of the month. Make sure that you visit early for the best selection.

The same software that runs the major coupon-printing sites often powers the individual printable coupons found on manufacturer websites. If you see bricks.coupons.com in your browser's address bar, for example, you'll know that coupon is powered by Coupons.com and it's a legitimate coupon that should print with the software you already loaded at Coupons.com. Once you've loaded the software from the four major sites, you'll be able to print most coupons you find online.

Note that when you want to print your second copy of a coupon, these sites work differently. On sites whose addresses start with bricks.coupons.com, individual coupons powered by Coupons.com, you can just hit the Back button on your browser a few times to print again. With individual coupons powered by SmartSource, you'll need to go back and click the coupon link again; hitting the Back button gives you an error.

Other manufacturers choose to release their coupons in Adobe Acrobat format, or PDF. In order to open and print PDF coupons, you need free Adobe Reader software; this is built into the original install on most computers, but if you don't have it already, you can download Reader at get.adobe.com/reader.

Using Adobe Acrobat is cheaper for manufacturers because they don't have to pay for the use of one of the major coupon-printing sites; however, PDF coupons lack controls. For example, every copy of a printed PDF coupon is identical to every other copy. This means that manufacturers have no way of preventing consumers from making multiple photocopies of these types of coupons or printing them unlimited numbers of times. They also have no way of preventing them from saving them to their hard drives or sharing them with all of their friends, so high-value coupons intended as one-time rewards often end up spiraling out of control.

HEADS-UP

Stores are somewhat leery of PDF-printed coupons, since they lack the unique dot-scan barcodes or other unique identifiers seen on coupons from major sites. Some stores refuse to take them at all, and if this is in their written coupon policy, you have little recourse but to use these coupons elsewhere.

Many manufacturers do choose to release their coupons in PDF format, however, and they're perfectly legitimate when put out by that manufacturer. When printing PDF coupons, always make sure that you received them directly from the manufacturer via e-mail or from the manufacturer's own website. This helps ensure that you don't get taken in by the fraudulent coupons that sometimes circulate online.

Store Website Coupons

Stores often release printable coupons on their websites. These can be either store coupons or manufacturer coupons, and in some cases, it's impossible to tell which until you print it out.

Target, for instance, always has a number of printable coupons on its site (coupons.target.com) and releases a new batch every week or two. There is nothing on the site, however, to indicate which coupons are Target coupons and which are manufacturer coupons. When you print out the coupons, they either say "Target web coupon" or "Manufacturer coupon" on the top, and their barcodes look different. Target web coupons are store coupons that are redeemable only at Target, while manufacturer coupons printed from the Target site can be used at any store that accepts printables.

Check to see if your local stores offer printable coupons. Visit their websites and look for a link to "coupons" or "savings." Also be sure to sign up for e-mail lists at the stores you most often shop, since they often share printable coupons with their subscribers you wouldn't otherwise see. Look for a link on their website that says something like: sign up for e-mails, sign up for our newsletter, or sign up for savings.

Some stores also offer bonus coupons just for signing up: Kohl's, for example, offers a printable coupon for $5 off any in-store purchase to all new e-mail subscribers. That's worth the minute it takes to sign up!

Coupons on Social Media Sites

Companies often release their highest-value coupons on Facebook—and many have even been offering limited-time coupons for free products for their Facebook fans. Why Facebook? Manufacturers can require you to "like" them or to load an app in order to print a coupon, which translates into future free marketing for them.

When you like a company's page on Facebook, you're giving the company permission to market to you that way in the future. It's as if you were adding them as a friend on Facebook, and their status updates show up on your home page right alongside the updates from all your friends. Further, when your friends see that you like a company on Facebook, it raises the odds that they will also like that company, increasing its market base even further.

Companies know that we increasingly tune out advertising. We often DVR or TiVo our TV programs and fast-forward through the commercials. We block or tune out banner ads on websites, and couldn't tell you a minute later what product we just saw advertised. When an update for a company or product shows up in our Facebook stream, it's harder to tune out and we're likely to pay more attention.

TIPS AND TRICKS

You only have to "like" a company or load its app long enough to print the coupon or request a free sample or other offer. If you don't want to see continued marketing messages from them, you simply need to "unlike" them on their Facebook page or remove their app under the privacy settings in your account when you are done. (Check out Facebook's help section for more specific instructions on how to do this.)

You can set up a dummy Facebook account just to print coupons and request freebies from companies. This keeps your personal Facebook separate from these businesses, or is a good option for people who have no use for Facebook otherwise.

Some companies and stores also release coupons on Twitter, but this is rarer. Again, you can set up a Twitter account just for this purpose, but often you're able to access their coupon links on Twitter without actually having to create an account or "follow" the company on Twitter.

Beyond manufacturers, stores also occasionally release store coupons on social networking sites like Facebook and Twitter. Grocery stores like Safeway have released produce coupons, for example, while Walgreens has offered coupons for free photos and $5 off a $25 purchase. You might want to like or follow your favorite stores to see what they have to offer.

The Least You Need to Know

- You can find hundreds of coupons online, often of higher value or unique coupons you don't see in Sunday coupon inserts.

- You need to install coupon-printing software for all of the major sites—but only once—then you should be set for printing any coupons you find online.

- Take advantage of manufacturer or store website coupons and e-mail newsletters for additional savings.

- Get your social on: companies release their best coupons on Facebook or Twitter, so get social and see what savings you can find.

Debunking Couponing Myths

In This Chapter

- The truth behind saving with everyday low prices
- The truth about the return on couponing investment
- The truth behind unhealthy couponing behaviors
- The truth behind couponing and ethical conduct

There are some common misconceptions about couponing, and portrayals of couponers in the popular media just feed into these stereotypes: "Everyone" knows that coupons are only for overly processed junk food. Everyone knows that couponing leads to obsessive hoarding and that couponers clear entire shelves and leave nothing for others. Everyone knows that you can save more simply by buying generics or shopping warehouse clubs.

Well luckily for us, "everyone" isn't always right. In this chapter, find out the real truth behind common couponing myths.

Save More at Everyday-Low-Price Stores?

People often don't take the time to coupon because of the popular idea that you can always save more just by shopping at discount stores or warehouse clubs, so why bother? As you're starting to see, this is far from the truth: when you match up coupons with sale prices and are strategic about your shopping trips, couponing almost always saves you more.

There are a few exceptions, though, where shopping at warehouse clubs or discount stores can actually help you save. We'll talk about some of these in the following sections.

Warehouse Clubs

Shoppers who prefer Sam's Club, Costco, or BJ's believe that the everyday savings at warehouse clubs trump any possible savings you can score at *high/low* grocery or drugstores by using coupons. If you're getting an economy-sized jar or pallet of products at a bulk discount price, the argument goes, then you're already saving plenty—so who needs coupons?

> **DEFINITION**
>
> **High/low** stores, such as regular chain grocery stores, tend to have *high* everyday prices, but *low* sale prices. Loss leaders and sales, especially when combined with coupons, lead to better savings at high/low stores (when you shop the sales) than at everyday low priced or warehouse stores—because these stores never hit the lows that high/low stores do.

This argument depends on comparing the everyday high prices at grocery or drugstores with everyday low prices at warehouse clubs and big box stores. When you compare everyday prices, yes, big box stores often (but not always!) win out.

But think back to the main keys to saving: stock up when items hit their rock-bottom price, and combine coupons with sales to save even more. While warehouse clubs are often the winner on everyday prices, they can't come close to touching the savings you'll see on good sale prices or loss leaders at grocery or drugstores. Costco doesn't generally do loss leaders. Sam's Club rarely does clearance. And these stores tend not to run sales, depending instead on that everyday-low-price formula.

Also, with the exception of BJ's, warehouse clubs don't accept manufacturer coupons. This means that you're at their pricing mercy, and can't use coupons to lower your out-of-pocket expense—or get items for free!

I did an experiment a little while back with diapers, which people often buy in bulk at warehouse clubs. The price for a box of Huggies Pull-Ups at my local Costco worked out to $.34 per diaper, while the regular price at my Walgreens worked out to $.47 per diaper. (It's kind of scary, when you think about it, what we spend on diapers!)

However, when I combined a sale at Walgreens with a coupon and a cash-back offer at the register (more on this in Chapter 7), I was able to buy two smaller packs of Huggies Pull-Ups for a cost of $.19 per diaper—and that's not even the best sale I've seen. I'd much rather stock up on smaller packages of diapers, for almost half the price of the boxes at the warehouse store.

To be fair, there are some items for which we less often see coupons that are good buys at warehouse clubs. Costco, for example, has some very nice bulk organic produce and cheap, large, rotisserie chickens. Bulk spices are often cheaper even after sales and coupons, because the markup at grocery stores is so incredibly high. (Ethnic markets are another great place to find cheap spices.) And in the absence of a sale elsewhere, warehouse-brand batteries are often more affordable.

Generic over-the-counter (OTC) medications—especially allergy pills like Loratadine (generic Claritin) and Cetirizine (generic Zyrtec)—are fantastic buys at warehouse clubs. A year's supply of Loratadine currently runs a little over $12 at Costco, which beats any possible coupon-plus-sale price for Claritin.

TIPS AND TRICKS

If you don't belong to a warehouse club, check Amazon.com for similar discounts on some warehouse club brands. As I type, for example, Kirkland-brand Loratadine (also sold at Costco) is available on Amazon for $12.65 for 365 pills, and Kirkland-brand Cetirizine is $15.95 for 365 tablets. If you've been considering joining a club for savings on items like allergy pills, check online first to see if you can get the savings without the annual fee.

You can also get your prescriptions filled at warehouse club pharmacies. By law, you don't have to be a member to use their pharmacy, and prescription prices there are often much cheaper than at the drugstores or grocery stores. Shop around!

Not a warehouse club member? Sam's Club offers free nonmember weekends a couple of times a year, and BJ's has offered a free trial for up to two months. Check club websites for free trial offers and stock up once or twice a year without paying an annual fee.

As with all your shopping, strategic purchases will help you save.

ALDI

ALDI is a growing chain that currently operates around 1,000 stores across 31 states. They tout themselves as a low-price alternative to regular grocery chains. With their $.25 shopping cart rentals, stores full of private-label brands, and charges for shopping bags, they say that customers can save up to 50 percent on their everyday grocery purchases.

> **TIPS AND TRICKS**
>
> One place ALDI shoppers can often save over regular grocery stores is on produce, especially in areas that lack ethnic or produce markets. In-season produce is often much cheaper there than at major grocery chains. Be aware, though, that you won't find organic produce, and you'll need to pay attention to the quality of what you buy.

Again, this "up to 50 percent savings" claim relies on matching everyday prices at regular grocery stores to everyday prices at ALDI (or at other competing discount generic stores). ALDI saves shoppers money by selling store brands and keeping stores small and variety low. Yet again, consumers can often do much better by shopping name-brand sales with coupons at regular stores.

Walmart

Walmart is a very interesting case. In 2011, they modified their official corporate coupon policy into one of the most liberal around (see more in Chapter 17). In practice, however, stores and cashiers follow official policy intermittently; shoppers sometimes have problems, for instance, using coupons that policy says they should accept, or using coupons on price-matched items. Realize that couponing at some Walmart locations will most likely require patience and self-assurance.

While Walmart is an everyday-low-price store whose sales don't touch the loss leaders at high/low stores, their price-match policy is what makes them competitive. Walmart will match prices on identical items from local competitors. If you have a Super Walmart near you, this is a great way to save on produce in particular, since you can collect local ads, bring them in, and get all the deals at once.

Target

Target, surprisingly, often beats the deals at Walmart, even though it has a reputation as a slightly more upscale chain. One of Target's main strengths lies in its printable store coupons (coupons.target. com), which can bring down the price of items nicely—or even make them free.

Target also has a price-matching policy, yet won't allow the use of Target store coupons on that matched price, which somewhat defeats the purpose. (They also won't match prices at stores that require loyalty cards, which leaves out most major grocery chains.) But if you have a SuperTarget near you, this is another great way to save on produce.

 HEADS-UP

Many Targets require you to price match at the service desk, rather than at the register. Talk to your local store to find out their policy.

Target also offers 5 percent off all purchases if you use their REDCard Visa or debit card (redcard.target.com/redcard/rc_main. jsp), but you can't currently use the debit card online.

Big Lots

Unlike discount stores like ALDI, Big Lots does have name-brand items at low prices. They're more of an overstock store, and their mix of items is hit or miss. Big Lots does not accept manufacturer coupons, which makes them less interesting for couponers. However, they do put out a weekly ad that often has name-brand items on sale. If you receive their ads in your paper or live near enough a store to pop in and grab one, you can bring it over to Walmart or Target, price match, and use your coupons there.

Save More By Buying Generic

Stores *love* this myth, and many put out handy comparison charts showing how much you'll save (generally, about 20 percent) by always buying the store or private-label brand over the competing name brand. Again, when coupons combined with sales can save you 50 to 90 percent off many name-brand products, these comparisons don't really hold up. You'll almost always do better shopping strategically for name-brand items than by stocking up on generics.

While the quality of some generics has improved in recent years, most of us do prefer name brands on many items—and sometimes for good reason! While generics do the job on some items, on others you're really paying for a difference in quality.

You Can't Really Save Much with Coupons

When you skim quickly through the Sunday newspaper's FSIs (free-standing inserts), it's easy to see how this myth takes hold. In some cases manufacturers have gotten stingy, sometimes offering almost-insulting coupons that are as low as $.25 off products normally priced at $5 and above. However, we have options that help us save more.

First, remember that online printable coupons are often much higher in value than those available in newspaper inserts. Watch for these higher-value coupons or search them out for products your family uses. Coupon values also vary over time—there may be a $1 coupon in this month's inserts, but a $2 coupon for the very same product in next month's inserts. Stock up when prices are lower with the higher-value coupon.

Secondly, wait to match up those coupons with sales. This is the most basic tenet of couponing: combine coupons with sale prices for maximum savings. Even if a coupon's face value seems low, its proportional value rises as the sale price of your item drops. And, if your local grocery store doubles coupons, those low-value coupons can also be much more valuable than they appear.

Lastly, think about switching to another brand. If one brand consistently has high prices and low-value coupons, check out the competition. Manufacturers are very aware of what their competition is doing, and when one drops its coupon values, another might put out a higher-value coupon. The more flexible you can be, the more you're able to save. (More on this in Chapter 5.)

The truth here is: you can really save with coupons if you plan to save and shop strategically around the sales.

Couponing Takes Too Much Time

The next common argument against couponing is that couponing takes too much time to be worth it. This is usually accompanied by an inflated sense of what someone's time is worth, such as "I could make $50 an hour if I were at work, so I'd be more productive spending my time working than couponing."

Is there something else you could be doing right this very second that will earn you as many dollars per hour? Go ahead, we'll wait. The rest of you, think about the potential rate of return here. If you can save your family hundreds of dollars per month just by investing a little bit of time into couponing and planning, that's huge. That's the difference between having to go back to work, being able to pay a little extra on some bills, making a car payment, or paying for braces.

Couponing doesn't have to be obsessive or time consuming. Will it take a bit more time to plan out shopping trips? Yes, but new tools and communities have really cut down on the time it takes, and the time you'll save by having staples on hand in your pantry makes it well worth your effort.

You can spend as little as 30 minutes a week planning and clipping your coupons, and still save big at the store. You can clip coupons in front of the TV at night; you can flip through your grocery store circulars while your baby is napping; you can otherwise use down time to plan out your trips. We'll talk in Chapters 8 and 16 about effective coupon strategies and planning your trips.

There Are No Coupons for Healthful Foods

Couponing is simply a tool. As with any tool, we can use it in many ways—sometimes for good, sometimes for ill. Yes, people can easily use coupons to fill entire carts with cheap candy and sodium-laden noodle bowls, but this is a choice. You don't have to buy that salty noodle bowl just because it's free with coupons (or, you can donate the free noodle bowl to others who can use it, if it's not part of your family's preferred diet).

Especially when you're new to couponing, it's easy to get carried away and buy everything you see, just because it's a deal. If it's not something your family needs or will use, it's not really a deal for you.

TIPS AND TRICKS

Look online for coupons for healthful foods. In the past month, I've printed coupons for salads, fresh pineapple, and berries, as well as for a number of name-brand organic products. None of these was available in my Sunday inserts.

Smart couponers use their savings in one area (say, health and beauty items or cereal) to shift their dollars toward their priorities in another area (say, produce and other whole foods). It's absolutely possible to coupon while still eating a healthful diet.

We'll talk later in this book about specific strategies for saving on healthful foods, and you'll find more on couponing for organic and whole foods in Chapter 17. Suffice it to say: there are coupons out there for meat, milk, produce, and organics. They're harder to find, but again, well worth the effort.

Couponing Leads to Hoarding

Like so many misconceptions about couponing, this myth is fed by popular portrayals of over-the-top couponers and excessive consumerism. It's important here to make the distinction between stockpiling (stocking up on a usable supply of items your family often uses when they hit their rock-bottom price) and hoarding (collecting items willy-nilly regardless of whether your family will use them).

Again, couponing is a tool. People can indeed use coupons to help them hoard items more cheaply. However not all couponers are hoarders—and most hoarders aren't couponers! True hoarders have a disorder, but providing for your family by planning ahead bears no resemblance to hoarding.

Effective Couponing Requires Acting Unethically

The rise of popular television shows featuring extreme couponers has brought couponing ethics to the forefront, because some of the couponers portrayed push the limits of the sport. Unfortunately, some people do choose to coupon in a less than ethical or less than kind manner. This hurts grocery stores and manufacturers, as well as the couponing community as a whole.

We can coupon ethically while still saving big, and should all keep in mind a few do's and don'ts.

Couponing Do's and Don'ts

We all make mistakes when we're new, but here are a few do's and don'ts to help keep yours to a minimum! Rules of thumb here include such basics as ...

- Never photocopy printable coupons, and don't buy them online—you don't know if someone else copied them.

- Only use one manufacturer's coupon per item.

- Don't use coupons for free products that come to you from friends' e-mail. These are most likely fakes.

- Don't clear entire store shelves—leave some for others.

When we use coupons illegitimately, it causes stores to crack down and gives couponers in general a bad name. Unfortunately, even bigger issues await.

First, know your store's policies and abide by them. "The customer is always right" doesn't apply to breaking the rules. Stores have different policies, so what you're able to do at one store, you're not always able to do at another. (Find more on store coupon policies in Chapter 16.)

Some bigger concerns, though, have come to light recently, as people go to extreme lengths to try to save. These stories range from people returning to the store multiple items that they purchased with coupons in order to get the cash, to people throwing blank slips of paper into the coupon slot at self-checkouts after scanning a legitimate coupon. These types of activities aren't couponing: they're out and out stealing.

Others are so anxious to save with coupons that they stoop to stealing Sunday coupon inserts out of newspaper boxes or their neighbors' newspapers.

In areas with high amounts of coupon theft, manufacturers have gone so far as to pull their coupons. The RedPlum coupon insert is now distributed only by mail in some areas rather than in newspapers, making it more difficult for legitimate couponers to find multiple copies of coupons.

Be Nice to Fellow Couponers

Couponers are a community, and we'll talk more in Chapter 15 about connecting with others online and off. Be willing to share your knowledge—and coupons!—with others. When you spot a great deal at your local store, your first impulse should be to share that information with others.

Couponing is more fun when you find a friend or two to join you on the journey, and you can swap ideas and coupons along the way. Have a friend with a dog but no baby? Have a baby but no pets? Trade your dog food coupons for her diaper coupons, and everyone wins.

Be Nice to Your Cashiers

You'll occasionally run into cashiers that are hostile to couponers because they think that their store loses money when you use coupons—but nothing could be further from the truth! Remember back in Chapter 2, we talked about the fact that manufacturer coupons work as a form of payment. Stores are reimbursed for the face value of the coupon, plus a handling fee for their trouble.

Stores that welcome couponers do well because their sales increase; the manufacturer is footing the bill for these coupons.

When you show up with a stack of coupons, recognize that you're making your cashier's job just that much harder. Her job is to get people through the line quickly, and you're slowing that process down a bit. (Not as much, though, as the person who fumbles for her checkbook or argues about prices or dithers about items already on the belt!)

So what can you do to make the process go more smoothly?

- Get everything organized before you get to the register; don't fumble for coupons while standing at the checkout.

- Make sure you haven't accidentally given her too many coupons or coupons for items you haven't purchased.

- If you have buy-one-get-one free (BOGO) coupons or free item coupons, put those products last on the belt for easy price checking.

- Make sure your coupons aren't expired, torn, or otherwise unusable.

- If she questions a coupon, make sure you're using it correctly—and don't get angry if she won't accept it. You can stop by the service desk on the way out if you don't feel the issue was resolved properly at checkout.

Remain pleasant and help the line move quickly, and your stores will get to know you as a good couponer.

The Least You Need to Know

- We more often save big with coupons and sales than at warehouse clubs or everyday-low-price stores.
- The small time and effort that couponing takes pays off huge at the register.
- Ethics are as important in couponing, as in the rest of life.

Using Coupons Effectively

Now that we've knocked out the basics, let's move on to Coupons 102. Once you start acquiring those coupons, how do you use them effectively, and what strategies will save you the most at the store? Build on that re-do of your shopping habits by embracing flexibility—try new brands, try new meals, and shop around your stockpile and the sales for maximum savings.

Then we'll take it a step further: how about getting paid back to shop? Learn how to trigger coupons for dollars off your next shopping trip, which you can use like cash toward anything at both grocery stores and drugstores.

Lastly, combine all these strategies to get items for pennies on the dollar—or often for free! Save your high-value coupons for sales, and use them on cheaper, smaller sizes to score free products. Learn when and how to use different types of coupons together to save multiple times on one item. And how to roll those money-back coupons at grocery stores and drugstores so that you can keep acquiring new dollars-off coupons without spending much out of your own pocket.

Embrace Flexibility

In This Chapter

- Trying different brands
- Shopping around for the best deal
- Planning your meals around sales and stockpiles

We're creatures of habit, so we easily fall into a comfortable pattern of shopping at the same stores, buying the same brands, and cooking the same meals. While habit is comforting, it can also be expensive: our favorite brands add up, our favorite stores may not be running a sale on the items we need, and our favorite meals might not match up with the grocery store deals this week.

The more flexible you can be in terms of both brands you buy and stores you shop at, the larger your potential savings. Remember we talked about loss leaders, or the items that stores put on huge discount in order to get people in the door? Well, this means that different stores have different items on sale each week. If you need peanut butter, but it's selling at your usual store for its usual (high) price this week, just drive a bit further down the street and shop at a competitor that has it on sale for $.99. If you always buy Jif but it's $2.99 this week, while Peter Pan is the loss leader for $.99, swallow your pride and your peanuts and give the other brand a try.

This chapter talks about maximizing your savings by embracing flexibility—and coming out richer in the process, both monetarily and personally.

Be Less Brand Loyal

Don't stop reading! You don't need to buy generic, and I'm not say-ing you need to give up *all* of your favorite brands ... just some of them, some of the time.

Here's why: Remember we talked about sales cycles, and the fact that products tend to hit their lowest price point about every three months? Well the brand that hits that low price point may not be your customary brand. You might always buy Kellogg's Raisin Bran, but Post Raisin Bran is on super-saver special this week; you might always buy Dawn liquid dish soap, but Palmolive is currently half the price of Dawn.

Try Post, try Palmolive, and start a relationship with some different brands that might turn out to be new family favorites.

> **TIPS AND TRICKS**
>
> Take a minute and think about the why behind what you buy. We're con-ditioned to pick up the same brands every time we go to the store. Is this the brand your mother bought? Is it just what you've always used? Is it at eye level and easy to grab? We don't always have good reasons for our buying choices; our brands have simply become habits.

You don't have to be disloyal to all of your favorites, but the more flexible you can be the higher potential savings you will realize at the register. We're essentially creatures of habit, and it can be hard to break out of our comfortable routines. Routine, however, does not help us save.

Pick a couple of favorites to be brand-loyal to—whether that's pop or peanut butter or pasta sauce—then give yourself permission to experiment among products in other areas.

Try New Product Offerings

You're more likely to see both deep discount pricing and high-value manufacturer coupons with new products. Let's say that Brand X has just come out with a new type of laundry detergent. You always buy Brand Y, which is usually priced higher than other brands, and generally has a sad little $.35 coupon in the Sunday coupon insert. You've put up with this because your mom always used Brand Y, and it's what you're used to seeing in your laundry room.

Brand X, though, really wants to promote their new product. There are sales all over town, you've clipped a high-value $2 coupon from the Sunday inserts, and there are more high-value coupons available online.

In this case, the potential savings from buying Brand X should more than outweigh your trepidation about trying something new. If you don't like it, that's okay; you didn't pay a lot to try it, and you don't ever have to buy it again! If you do like it, now you have another potential brand in your arsenal of choices, and a wider variety to pick from among any upcoming sales.

HEADS-UP

New product offerings often have the highest value coupons. Manufacturers have to get you to try a product before they can get you hooked, so they offer their best coupons on new or reformulated items. You'll score huge savings by being willing to try something new!

Over the past year, high-value new-product coupons combined with introductory sales have netted me everything from free dish liquid, to free fabric softener, to free ice cream bars. The dish liquid wasn't my favorite, but the extra free bottles went right over to my local food pantry—a win-win situation. The fabric softener works just fine, and it's lovely not to have to think about buying it and just shop from the little stash in my pantry. The ice cream? Well, that was to die for!

You Don't Have to Buy Generic

Don't worry! Being less brand loyal does not mean you have to buy generics. As a matter of fact, when you combine sales with coupons, you almost always get a better deal on the name brand than on its store-brand equivalent.

We talked about this myth in Chapter 4. How many coupons for generics do you see in your paper or online? While the everyday prices on generic products are often lower than the everyday prices on brand names, you don't see the super sales on these items that you do on name-brand products, nor do you see the coupons for these products.

Effective couponing involves shopping those super-low sales cycles, not shopping everyday prices. You'll still enjoy name-brand products—you're just now able to try a bigger variety of them.

You'll Find New Favorites

Trying new brands can actually help you find new favorites. In my precouponing days, we always bought Jif, just because … well, because we'd always bought Jif. One day the store was out of crunchy Jif, so I grabbed a jar of Skippy Natural Super Chunk instead. That night, my husband asked, "Did you buy a new brand of peanut butter? This is great!" Now, Skippy Natural is a recurring brand in our household—luckily for us, Skippy tends to put out coupons more often, and goes on sale more often than Jif.

As you start experimenting with different brands in different product categories, you'll often find that several brands work equally well or taste equally good, while others deserve a pass. You won't necessarily like every laundry detergent out there, but you'll probably find that several brands do equally well at getting your clothes clean. You won't necessarily like every brand of corn chips out there, but you might find that several have the acceptable balance of saltiness and crunchiness. You'll never know until you give it a try, and it can be fun to try something new.

Be Less Store Loyal

Just as brand loyalty ends up costing you in the long run, store loyalty can also end up making you pay more for the products you need. Just as sales cycles on individual items vary—sometimes it's a good week to buy Skippy, sometimes it really isn't—sales cycles at individual stores also vary. This week may be a great week to shop at Stop & Shop, but next week it may be a better week to shop at Shaw's. Shop around, and save.

COUPON QUIPS

Don't base your regular shopping trips on which store is prettier, or has better lighting, or has the cleanest bathrooms, or the newest carts; your bottle of ketchup is going to be the same bottle of ketchup no matter where you buy it.

Again, you don't have to stop shopping entirely at your favorite store, but be willing to shop around for better deals.

Shopping around also lets you find new coupons. Remember we talked in Chapter 2 about the different types of manufacturer coupons available in stores? Manufacturers often choose a single chain in a region in which to distribute their coupons: You'll find a certain blinkie machine in Safeway, but not in Albertsons. You'll see a tearpad in Winn-Dixie that you'd never find in Publix. Some stores also distribute coupon booklets that are only found in that store, but contain manufacturer coupons that can be used anywhere.

Whenever you pop into a new store, take a few minutes to look around for these. The more coupons you have in hand, the more savings you'll realize later.

Couponers in areas with a lot of stores nearby can cherry pick the deals, or go from store to store just to pick up the best loss leaders at each. You don't have to fill your whole cart at one store; you can pop in for quick trips at three stores and just pick up a few items from each one.

I often take a little drive down "grocery row," and pop into two or three stores just to snag the best loss leaders at each. It takes me about the same amount of time to do this as it does to do a large stock-up shopping trip at one store, but I come out much better in the long run.

If you don't want to drive around to multiple stores, you might want to just pick one grocery store and one drugstore each week to shop at, based on their current sales and your own needs.

> **TIPS AND TRICKS**
>
> If your local store is consistently out of stock on loss leaders, never fear. Stop by customer service to pick up a rain check, which allows you to purchase that product at its deeply discounted sale price at a later date when the store has had a chance to restock.
>
> Stores have different rain check policies: Some are good for 30 or 60 days, while others are indefinite. Others limit quantities, so they might only write you a rain check for 2, 4, or 6 identical items—but if they're still out of stock when you stop back in toward the end of the week, simply grab yourself another rain check if you had intended to buy more.

Shopping around for the deals is understandably more difficult to do if you live in an area with just one grocery store or without a lot of competition, especially with sky-high gas prices we're seeing these days. See Chapter 17 for more on couponing in rural areas.

Change It Up

Beyond buying the same brands and shopping at the same stores, we also tend to get into a pattern of cooking the same meals. This can end up costing us more than we expect when the ingredients we need aren't on sale or are out of season. Test this out the next time you go to the store: track what you are spending on products for just one family dinner, and you might be a bit shocked.

My local grocery store puts together endcaps of "$10 dinners" they tout as a bargain. They'll tell you, for example, to pick up pasta, salad, bread, and sauce for one low $10 price. Think this through: Spending $10 on dinner each night over the course of a month comes out to $300 a month—for dinner alone! That doesn't leave a lot of room in your budget for breakfast, lunch, household items, diapers ….

By combining coupons with sales, strategic shopping, and cooking, we can do much, much better.

Cook from Your Pantry

Once you're stocked up on the basics, you'll have weeks where you may need to pick up only milk and produce. Just cook from your pantry when there aren't good sales or when you need to start using up some of your stockpile. Think about how much you'll save if you simply avoid grocery shopping for a week.

In general though, instead of planning out your meals then going to the store to shop for ingredients, try switching it up: look in your pantry and freezer to see what you have in stock, then look at your store circulars to see what is on sale. You can then plan your meals around a combination of the ingredients you already have and what you can get cheaply at the store this week.

Browse recipe collections online and cookbooks at the library for new meal ideas, and have some fun with it! Sites like Allrecipes.com have a handy ingredient search. Open up your pantry, fridge, and freezer; plug in a few items you have; and see what they come up with for you.

TIPS AND TRICKS

When it comes to creative recipe combinations, Google can be your best friend. For example, I was recently looking at a bounty of serrano peppers from my garden, a couple of sad little limes leftover from margaritas, and a scrawny "sell by today" whole chicken I picked up last-minute at my local Dominick's (Safeway) for less than $2. A quick Google search ("serrano lime chicken recipe") and about an hour later, we were feasting on roasted chile-lime chicken courtesy of the Food Network (www. foodnetwork.com/recipes/aida-mollenkamp/roasted-chile-lime-chicken-recipe/index.html). This recipe has now become a new family favorite.

While we still do have a collection of old, tried-and-true family recipes, this is now ever-expanding as we find new family favorites. This is a win-win situation: we're spending less on food than ever before, we're finding new favorites and new flavors, cooking has become more fun, and the kids are becoming less picky as their palate becomes more varied.

Mix It Up

You can also cook from your pantry by modifying family favorites. I once picked up several bags of Craisins off the clearance shelf and, after we ate our fill, wondered what to do with them. Craisins instead of raisins turned out to be great in an oatmeal cookie recipe, added to homemade trail mix, and sprinkled on top of some (free-after-coupon) instant oatmeal! Think creatively about the ingredients you have on hand.

Meal Planning

One place to be less flexible is on meal planning. We've all been there: You get home at 6:00 and stare blindly into the fridge, hoping that dinner has somehow planned itself while you were gone. When nothing materializes, you end up ordering pizza, or Chinese, or swinging through the drive-thru.

When we don't think ahead about what we're going to eat this week, we end up spending more on impulse dinners and fast food. Plan out a week's worth of dinners around your stockpile and the sales *before* doing your weekly grocery shopping, and make sure you have all the ingredients on hand. (It's a great idea to plan a couple of nights of leftovers in there, too.)

Freezer Cooking

If you really want to plan ahead, another way to save on meals—and save your sanity!—is to think about the idea of freezer cooking. Some people do a big monthly day of cooking where they stock their freezer with anywhere from 10–30 dinners. It's less intimidating to start small; once or twice a week, double a recipe and make a second batch to freeze.

This not only saves time, it saves money. When you have precooked meals waiting for you, it's much easier just to heat one up than to figure out dinner from scratch. This can help you avoid last-minute carryout or pizza nights on busy days when you don't have time to plan.

TIPS AND TRICKS

Store your prepared meals in freezer bags for easy stacking. Label each with the meal name and date, and be sure to rotate occasionally so that the older meals are on top and toward the front.

If you don't want to freeze entire meals, you'll also save time and money just by doing some of the prep work ahead of time. Big sale on ground beef at the store this week? Buy extra, cook it up, and freeze meal-sized batches in quart-sized freezer bags. You then have browned beef ready for chili, tacos, and other meals later in the month. Big sale on veggies? Chop up and freeze easy starters like green peppers, onions, carrots, hot peppers, and more, then pull them out for easy meal prep later.

You can freeze most meals, but for specific freezer recipes, tips, meal plans, and once-a-month cooking recipes check out Once a Month Mom (onceamonthmom.com) and Money Saving Mom (moneysavingmom.com/downloads/freezer-cooking-planners). Also check your library for classic cookbooks like *Once-a-Month Cooking* or *Fix, Freeze, and Feast*, and *The Complete Idiot's Guide to Easy Freezer Meals* for more ideas on bulk freezer cooking.

Swap with Friends

Think about setting up a dinner swap with a friend. Let's say you cook a double batch of dinner two nights a week … she cooks a double batch of dinner two nights a week … and you swap! Make sure if you try this that you have similar tastes and budgets; you don't want one family to feel they're expending more money and energy, or to swap recipes your kids just won't eat. Talk about it ahead of time so that you don't end up swapping lasagna for lasagna and to make sure that you're on the same page.

The Least You Need to Know

- Sticking with the same brands puts a big dent in your coupon savings. Mix it up, and maximize savings.
- If your regular store lacks good sales, mix it up there, too. Check out another store where the deals are hopping.
- Set yourself up for savings success by working your meal plans around sales and your own stockpile.

Money-Back Coupons and Rewards Programs

In This Chapter

- Catalinas—coupons for money off your next shopping trip—sometimes print out at the register when you buy qualifying items
- Rules and restrictions apply when qualifying for and redeeming Catalinas
- Many stores and companies run their own rewards programs

What's better than buying items for pennies on the dollar? Being paid to take items out of the grocery store, of course! Coupons that print out after your transactions sometimes offer savings off your next shopping trip that you can use to buy anything in the store. Yes, you can use them to pay for your meat, pay for your produce, or pay for any of your other favorite items that seldom go on sale—it's like having extra cash in your pocket, that you've earned just by shopping.

Want more ways to get rewards for shopping? Other stores (and restaurants) run rewards programs attached to their loyalty cards that reward you over time for purchases, or for buying particular items. Be sure to investigate the programs that are available at your local stores. When you get money back at the store, you're really learning to save big, and this chapter lets you know how to get started.

Catalina Coupons

Many grocery stores have separate machines near the registers that print out what are known as Catalinas (also referred to as YourBucks), named after Catalina Marketing Corporation, which supplies the machines and runs the program. These Catalina coupons vary in type: They may be ...

- A manufacturer coupon for a particular item.

- A store coupon for a particular item.

- A store coupon for a dollar amount off your next order of *$X or more* (such as $5 off of your next $50 purchase).

- An advertisement for an upcoming or ongoing promotion.

- A coupon for a local noncompeting service business.

- A coupon for a dollar amount off your next shopping trip.

Couponers, though, often use the general term Catalinas to refer specifically to coupons for a dollar amount off your next shopping trip—because these are the most fun!

Catalina machines near the registers at drug and grocery stores print coupons both for specific items and for dollars off your next shopping order at the store.
(Courtesy of Catalina Marketing)

Shoppers often ignore these coupons because they don't know what they are, or how valuable they can be. Since the Catalina machines also print out advertisements ($19.99 oil changes! Get cash back with Discover!), we get used to thinking of these coupons as ads we should just toss out, rather than potential high-value coupons we should keep.

Always reading your Catalinas can pay off. I've sometimes found high-value Catalina coupons just lying around in grocery store carts, in the parking lot, or on the floor, because people who originally received them didn't know the value of what they were getting. So always be sure to look at yours to see what coupons you may have received.

Catalina Triggers

So what makes these oh-so-useful Catalina coupons print out? Different types of Catalinas have different triggers. While some seem random, the dollars-off-your-next-order Catalina coupons are triggered when you purchase a specific item or combination of items.

HEADS-UP

Keep an eye on the Catalina machine to see if anything prints out. While it beeps to let your cashier know to hand you the coupon, sometimes they don't notice or have already moved on to the next customer.

It's especially useful to know before you go what might trigger a dollars-off-your-next-shopping-trip Catalina, so you can plan your purchases to maximize your money-back coupons.

Cents-Off

When it comes to a cents-off Catalina coupon for a particular item, these often print out when you buy that item, as a reward, or when you buy a competing item, to try and entice you to switch. (Sometimes, however, these seem to be random and not tied to anything else in your order.)

Know your store's policies before you go. Some stores accept all manufacturer Catalina coupons for a specific item, even if they sport another store's logo. Others only accept manufacturer Catalina coupons that printed out at that same store. Store Catalina coupons are only redeemable at the same store where you received them.

Take these cents-off coupons and file them away with the rest of your manufacturer coupons as you wait for a sale.

Off Your Next Shopping Trip

What triggers a Catalina coupon for X dollars–off your next shopping trip? Manufacturers run these promotions regularly, either at specific grocery stores or nationally across most stores with Catalina machines. It's the manufacturer's call when and where to run their promos, and these are not often well advertised by stores. So here are some ways to help you keep track of these types of promos.

Start with your local grocery store ads. Although they don't tend to include all the current Catalina deals, especially the smaller single-item promos, they often give you a list of some of the participating items in multi-item Catalina promotions.

You also want to keep an eye out for information in the store itself. Look for shelf tags announcing money-back offers. There's so much signage in grocery stores that we tend to tune it all out, but white or yellow shelf tags under participating items often provide information about ongoing Catalina promos. Sometimes these are also advertised on the products themselves; I've found peelies on Kraft cheese, for example, giving details on a Kraft Catalina promotion.

Read any Catalina alerts that print out in store. In addition to printing coupons and ads, Catalina machines also sometimes print alerts about upcoming promos, especially when you buy one of the brands or items that will be included. Your alerts will let you know what items you need to buy on a future date in order to receive your Catalina.

While you keep your eyes open in the store, also check online before making your trip; start with Coupon Network (www.couponnetwork.com). In addition to printable grocery coupons, Coupon Network also provides information on some, but not all, of these Catalina promotions.

In order to see details on these promos, you'll need to create an account at Coupon Network so they know what stores you shop at. Then click the "YourBucks Offers" tab on the top right to see a list of ongoing Catalina promotions; click on any item in the list to see more details and a list of participating retailers.

In order to see the complete information on any Catalina listed on Coupon Network, you'll need to log in to your Coupon Network account and print out the information on each offer you're interested in. This is currently the only way to see specific start and end dates for Catalina offers, as well as the full information on tiered Catalinas. (Tiered Catalinas give you increasing rewards as you buy more items in a single transaction; they might give you $2 off your next order for buying two participating items, $3 off for buying three, and $4 off for buying four or more, for example.)

Catalina promotions run for a set period of time, sometimes for a week or two, and other times as long as a month. Sometimes these are single-item promotions, such as: "buy two Skippy peanut butter, get $1 off your next shopping order," and sometimes these are multi-item promotions, such as: "buy $25 in participating ConAgra products, get $10 off your next shopping order" or "buy any five participating products, get $5 off your next shopping order."

Precoupon

The best thing about Catalinas is that they trigger on your premanufacturer coupon purchases. Remember, manufacturer coupons are a form of payment for your items, so it doesn't matter whether you pay using those or pay using cash; your Catalina prints regardless. We'll talk more about maximizing your Catalina rewards by pairing these deals with coupons in Chapter 8.

Catalina Caveats

While Catalina coupons for a dollar amount off your next shopping trip can be used in the store much like cash, they are not exactly cash, and there are some important differences. You'll need to be aware of a few restrictions and caveats. Other than these, though, you can use your Catalinas to score yourself some free groceries, and that makes them incredibly valuable.

Catalinas Expire

First, Catalinas are coupons, so they do have expiration dates. Those that are for a dollar amount off your next shopping trip generally expire one to two weeks from the date they print. Don't let these expire! If you do, it's like you're throwing money in the trash.

No Tax, No Change

Since Catalinas are coupons, they cannot be used to pay sales tax, and you can't get change back from your Catalina. So, for instance, you can't use a $5-off-your-next-shopping-trip Catalina to buy a $3 item, and expect to get back $2 in cash. Note the wording on these, your Catalina will say something like: "$5 off your next shopping trip of $5 or more," meaning that you can't use it on a shopping trip of $4.99 or less—it just won't go through.

Restrictions Apply

Catalinas are also not exactly like cash because the fine print on these coupons always lists a number of exclusions. For instance, you can't use them to buy things like lottery tickets, gift cards, or postage stamps. At some chains, oddly enough, Catalinas can't even be used to purchase dairy items.

What If Your Catalina Doesn't Print?

Successful Catalina prints depend on everything aligning just right. Since the Catalina machine is a separate system from the store's cash register, information on your transaction is transmitted via satellite to Catalina, which bounces back information on what you should receive at the register. Sometimes the satellite is down, or your store's Catalina system is down and needs a good reboot. Also avoid doing Catalina shopping between about 11 p.m. and 3 a.m., as the system goes down sometime in there to load updates each night.

TIPS AND TRICKS

If a Catalina doesn't print that you know you were entitled to, wait until the next day, then call Catalina Marketing at 1-888-8COUPON and give them the information off your receipt; they should be able to replace your Catalina via postal mail.

If you're shopping in anticipation of receiving a Catalina, check the machine before you start your transaction—look for a solid green light. A red light is bad; a blinking light is bad—this means that the machine is down, out of paper, jammed, or otherwise not printing. Switch to another lane and save yourself some hassle.

If after all that your Catalina fails to print, start with customer service at your store. If the Catalina is advertised in the ad or on the shelf, point to the ad and show that you purchased the appropriate product(s). Sometimes they can force the Catalina to print for you.

Store Rewards Programs

Many stores—not just drug and grocery stores—offer their own loyalty programs that let you earn rewards and benefit from special coupons and discounts for registered users. Here are a few examples, but check other stores you often frequent to see if they offer similar programs.

Department Stores

The large conglomerate of Kmart, Sears, The Great Indoors, and Lands' End uses a single Shop Your Way Rewards card (shopyourwayrewards.com), and rewards can be earned and redeemed at any member store. You earn 10 points for every dollar you spend, both online and in store. For each 1,000 points you earn, you get $1 credit you can spend online or in store. They also run special promos where you can earn double rewards on certain dates at certain stores.

Department stores like JC Penney also run their own rewards programs (www.jcprewards.com). Earn 1 point for each dollar you spend (with a bonus for using a JCP credit card), and 250 points gets you a $10 reward.

Office Supply Stores

Office supply stores each run their own rewards program. These offer points for specific in-store purchases (often ink, toner, paper, and copy services), which you can redeem as in-store credit.

Each also offers special bonus rewards offers in weekly ads, which work like rebates—you receive a certain dollar amount or the whole purchase price of the item back as rewards. At each store, you can also recycle used ink or toner cartridges for rewards credit.

Since each program is so similar, I'll just tell you where to sign up for each—pick the store or stores near you and read about the benefits they offer:

- Staples—www.staplesrewardscenter.com
- Office Max—www.officemaxperks.com (There is a general rewards program and one for teachers.)
- Office Depot—myworkliferewards.com

When you sign up for rewards, you'll also start to receive store coupons via e-mail and postal mail.

TIPS AND TRICKS

Some office supply stores will take competitor coupons. If one store is more convenient to you, sign up for rewards programs and e-mail coupons at all three. Ask your local store for their policy.

Rewards generally become available to use the next quarter, and you may need to hit a minimum balance in your account.

Pet Supplies Stores

Pet supplies stores also offer perks to loyal rewards card customers, such as printable and mailed coupons, as well as in-store discounts for using your loyalty card.

- PetCo—petco.com/Pals/PalsLogin.aspx
- PetSmart—customer-support.petsmart.com/pet-perks

Be sure to register your card online for additional benefits and e-mail offers.

Bookstores

Barnes & Noble runs a rewards card program, for which they do charge $25 a year. Their card offers you 10 percent off most purchases, free express shipping on online orders, and 40 percent off hardcover bestsellers. Do the math and see if it's worth it to you, depending on your shopping patterns.

Books-a-Million runs a similar member rewards program at $20 a year, which offers 10 percent off all online purchases as well as additional discounts in retail stores.

- Barnes & Noble—www.bn.com/u/Membership-Join/ 379002828
- Books-a-Million—www.booksamillion.com/product/ MEMBERSHIP

When you sign up, you also receive e-mail coupons for use both online and in store.

Restaurants

We'll talk more about savings on dining out in Chapter 11, but some restaurants do run their own loyalty card rewards programs. Here are just a couple of examples.

Panera

Grab a free MyPanera card in store, then register it online at mypanera.panerabread.com. They've been giving out a free pastry just for signing up. Use your card every time you visit to accrue random rewards ranging from $1–$2 off a menu item, to a free drink or pastry.

You cannot choose your own rewards, and they won't necessarily reward you with items you always buy. However the random freebies and savings potential make it worth signing up, especially if you visit regularly.

Starbucks

At starbucks.com/card, register any gift card online and it becomes a Starbucks rewards card. You get instant rewards such as a free drink on your birthday and free refills in store, plus accrue rewards such as a free drink coupon for every 15 drinks you buy. If you have a morning coffee habit and pick up Starbucks on the way to work, register a card and reap the rewards.

Product Rewards Programs

Beyond specific stores, some companies reward you for brand loyalty with their own rewards programs on specific products. Save up points by going online to enter codes from products, and then redeem your points for gift cards or merchandise. Representative examples include:

- MyCokeRewards—www.mycokerewards.com
- Huggies Enjoy the Ride—www.huggies.com/en-US/rewards
- Pampers Gifts to Grow—giftstogrow.com
- Tropicana Juicy Rewards—juicyrewards.tropicana.com

Check the products you buy the most to see if they have an associated rewards program.

The Least You Need to Know

- Catalina coupons for specific items or for a dollar amount off your next shopping trip print from machines by the register.
- High-value Catalina coupons are like free money to use toward anything in the store.
- Store loyalty programs can pay off with store credit and high-value coupons.

Drugstore Savings

In This Chapter

- Save big with drugstore promos, coupons, and money-back offers
- Walgreens Register Rewards and special rules
- CVS Extra Bucks rewards and promos
- Rite Aid +UP rewards, rebates, and promos
- Look for prescription savings and coupons at the drugstore and beyond

We've talked a lot about saving on food at the grocery store, but drugstores offer their own special brand of savings opportunities. This is where you can combine coupons with sales and money-back rewards to score many of your toiletries and over-the-counter medications for free, which adds up to hundreds in saving for the average family.

In this chapter, learn ways to maximize your savings and walk away with free items at three major U.S. drugstore chains: Walgreens, CVS, and Rite Aid. We'll also talk about the basics of saving on prescriptions.

Shop for Free at Your Local Drugstore

BC (Before Couponing), I almost never shopped at my local drug-stores; their prices were just too high for my blood. But just as at the grocery store, drugstores are high/low stores where everyday prices are outrageous, but sale prices combined with coupons and money-back offers can get you over-the-counter medication plus health and beauty items for free—or at least, for cheap! You'll want to coupon with the loss leaders at drugstores, just as you do at grocery stores.

Each major drugstore chain runs its own money-back rewards program, and offers both weekly and monthly deals. Weekly deals are listed in each Sunday's ad, while monthly deals are often only advertised on shelf tags in the store—or sometimes not advertised at all.

Walgreens

The Register Rewards program at Walgreens is run by the same company that maintains the Catalina coupon program at grocery stores, Catalina Marketing, and the rewards coupons that print out at Walgreens are technically Catalina coupons. Register Rewards, however, have their own special rules and quirks, so you'll need to understand those going in.

No Rolling

Walgreens' Register Rewards (RR) do not roll. This means that if you use the RR you receive from buying an item to buy another of that same item (or even another item from the same manufacturer, which will be listed on the RR), you will not receive a new RR for purchasing that item.

TIPS AND TRICKS

How do you know what items are producing RR each week? Walgreens puts out a weekly ad each Sunday that lists weekly RR deals and your final price after RR.

Say what? Let's use an example. For instance, let's say that Walgreens this week is offering $5 back in RR when you purchase a Gillette Fusion ProGlide razor. So you walk in, buy your razor, and duly receive your RR coupon for $5 off your next shopping order at Walgreens.

You then decide you want a second Gillette Fusion ProGlide razor. You might think: "Hey, if I use my $5 coupon to pay for it, I can pay less out of pocket and get myself a shiny new $5 RR to use." Unfortunately, though, if you use your $5 RR from buying your first Gillette Fusion ProGlide as part of your payment for your second Gillette Fusion ProGlide, that new RR simply will not print.

Fortunately, Walgreens offers multiple RR–producing opportunities each week. So let's say you really want that second razor. One thing you could do to minimize your out-of-pocket cost is to look for another RR–producing item to roll your $5 coupon into.

For the purposes of our example, we'll pretend that this week Walgreens also has a RR deal going on Degree deodorant: buy two for $5, get a $4 RR. So you now can use your $5 RR from buying your Gillette razor to pay for your two Degree deodorants and earn yourself a shiny new $4 RR—which you can then roll right into a second razor. You minimize your out-of-pocket cost when you roll your RR between different RR–producing items.

One Item, One Coupon

Register Rewards are manufacturer coupons. At Walgreens, the number of manufacturer coupons you use in one transaction, including your RR, has to be less than or equal to the number of items in your order. Each manufacturer coupon, including RR, needs its own item to "attach" to.

What does this mean? Let's go back to our Gillette Fusion ProGlide razor example, and pretend it's on sale this week for $9.89. You have a $4 RR from buying Degree deodorant, and you also have a $4 manufacturer coupon for Gillette that you clipped out of your Sunday paper. Unfortunately, you can't just buy the razor and use both of these coupons on it, because the Walgreens registers see that as using two manufacturer coupons on one item. If you want to use both coupons, you will need to add a filler item to your order—a small low-cost item for your RR to "attach" to.

In this case, let's say you buy a Gillette Fusion ProGlide razor along with a $.35 caramel from the basket by the register. Now you have two items in your shopping trip, so you are able to use both your $4 manufacturer coupon for Gillette and your $4 RR coupon—even though the value of that RR is well over the item it is attaching to.

COUPON QUIPS

This one-per-item limitation only applies to manufacturer coupons. You can use as many store coupons as you want, including the in-ad coupons; the one-coupon-per-item rule is only when you're using RR or other manufacturer coupons.

At Walgreens, a multi-item coupon (such as a $1/2 coupon) tends to attach to both items, so it counts as a coupon for both. When it comes to buy-one-get-one free (BOGO) coupons, they will often also attach to both items, so you may want to throw something else small into your order just to be safe.

One Per Transaction

Only one Register Rewards will print per offer per transaction. Back to our Gillette Fusion ProGlide example: Again, it's on sale this week for $9.89, and you get back $5 RR for buying one. Let's say you buy two in one transaction for $19.78—you'll still only receive one $5 RR, even though you're buying two razors. In order to receive two $5 RR, you need to split your razor purchases up into two separate transactions.

In an effort to keep items in stock, some stores do limit the number of like RR transactions per customer to one or two—especially on hot deals where an item is free after RR.

Store Coupons

Walgreens releases a new set of store coupons each week in its ad, as well as a monthly coupon booklet that can be found on stands at the front of the store by the weekly ads. They also release special thematic coupon booklets, such as beauty, infant care, or allergy booklets, with additional coupons. These are harder to find, and might not be available in all stores.

At Walgreens, a store coupon applies to each qualifying item in your order. Let's say you have an in-ad coupon for $1 off of Neosporin. If you buy two Neosporin in one transaction, just one store coupon will take $1 off each of them, for a total of $2.

You also don't need to tear coupons out of the ad or Walgreens booklets. Since these come off as a store discount at the register, cashiers don't need to keep the coupon—they can scan it right out of your ad.

TIPS AND TRICKS

Can't find the Walgreens coupon booklet people are talking about? Coupon-friendly Walgreens will sometimes punch in the coupon number for you, which you can get from a friend or find listed on coupon blogs online. (More on these in Chapter 15.) Since they don't need to keep the coupon, this works just as well. If you develop a relationship with a coupon-friendly store, they'll be good to you.

Lastly, Walgreens offers irregular printable coupons online. These are most often friends and family discount coupons for 15 percent off your entire order (20 percent off Walgreens brand), or $5 off a $25 purchase. Sign up for Walgreens e-mails on their site to stay informed about these offers.

CVS

Walgreens is not the only game in town, which is good for couponers because competition always leads to better deals and prices! CVS runs its own money-back program, but theirs works a bit differently.

At CVS, their money-back rewards program is not run by Catalina. Extra Bucks rewards, which are like cash back and good toward anything else in the store, print out on your receipt as store coupons tied to your personal loyalty card. ExtraCare Bucks (ECB) also accrue on quarterly purchases and prescriptions; you receive a $1 ECB for every two prescriptions you fill, and 2 percent back on your postcoupon quarterly spending. Prescription and quarterly ECB print out at the beginning of each quarter, while weekly ECB rewards print out at the register when you purchase qualifying items.

Unlike Walgreens Register Rewards, ECB are store coupons and can only be used at CVS. These are also tied to your particular CVS card, so if you receive an ECB reward or a store coupon that prints out at the price scanner or register, it will only work for your card. (This also means that if you find someone else's ECB lying around in a cart leave them be, unlike with generic Register Rewards and Catalinas, you won't be able to use them yourself.)

Since ECB are store coupons, you can use as many as you want per transaction, and don't need to worry about them attaching to an item as you do with Register Rewards at Walgreens. These also adjust down—so if you want to use a $3 ECB to purchase a $2.99 item, they'll just scan your ECB at $2.99.

Rolling

ECB always roll. This means you can use them to purchase the same ECB-generating item (as long as you don't hit the posted limit), or to buy any other ECB-generating item, and they'll still generate new ECB.

Each ECB offer at CVS has a limit, which will be listed in the weekly ad. These limits are per card, so if the ad says "limit 2," that means only two ECB will print for that particular qualifying item or items from the same CVS card. While Walgreens controls its deals by preventing rolling, CVS controls its deals by per-card limits.

Because they control deals by card, you can spread your ECB-producing purchases across more than one visit; you don't have to purchase them all in one transaction. Let's say you need to hit $15 in participating products to generate a $5 ECB reward. If your store only has a couple of products left in stock, you can purchase just $7.50 worth of products. CVS keeps track of these purchases on your card, and then you can purchase the additional $7.50 in qualifying items at another store, or later in the week.

If your store is out, CVS will also write rain checks that include the ECB for ECB-producing items. (Walgreens won't write rain checks with RR attached, only for the sale price.)

Some people do sign up for multiple cards in order to do the same deal multiple times. CVS, however, is beginning to crack down on this practice and enforce one-card-per-household limits.

Store Coupons

Always scan your card at their in-store price scanner/coupon center (what couponers like to call the "magic coupon machine!") because bonus coupons print out there. Keep scanning until it says no coupons available, because sometimes it prints more than one set. This machine is usually located at the front of the store near the registers; larger stores may have a second machine back by the pharmacy.

TIPS AND TRICKS

Be sure to sign up for CVS ExtraCare e-mails with your card number (www. cvs.com/CVSApp/user/extracare/extracare.jsp) and you'll get a bonus $4 off a $20 purchase printable coupon, plus random e-mail coupons throughout the year. The cool thing about CVS? Your $4/$20 and other $/$$ coupons can be used before any other store or manufacturer coupons, which can make for great deals.

Local newspapers across the country often run $5/$20 CVS store coupons. If you're planning a trip to CVS, it's sometimes worth the expense to buy the paper in order to score that coupon—if you spend $1 to buy the specific paper containing a $5/$20 coupon, but then go and use that coupon at CVS, you're still ahead $4.

Bonus Clubs and Programs

Earn extra ECB at CVS by signing up for one or more of their special clubs. To sign up for these, simply go online and enter your ExtraCare card number on the CVS website, or ask in store.

The ExtraCare Beauty Club rewards members with a 10 percent off beauty purchase coupon for joining, e-mail coupons for beauty products, and a bonus $5 ECB reward for every $50 spent on beauty items—precoupon! Sign up and start getting your $5 ECB rewards without even thinking about it, because these qualifying purchases range from cosmetics to hair care products.

ExtraCare Advantage for Diabetes rewards members with double ECB on over 100 items, plus special coupons for diabetes-related products that are either e-mailed or print out at the coupon center in store.

At CVS, also invest in what they call a "green bag tag" for $.99. Attach it to your reusable shopping bag, and on every fourth shopping trip that they scan your tag, you get a bonus $1 in ECB. (Note: you'll only get the credit for one trip per card per day.)

Rite Aid

Rite Aid rounds out the big three drugstore chains with its +UP rewards program. Use your Rite Aid wellness+ loyalty card to buy qualifying products, and earn dollar-off coupons for your next Rite Aid shopping trip. As with CVS, these are store coupons that print on your receipt—and, like at CVS, you can roll them into the same offer and still receive new +UP rewards. Unlike at CVS, they will not adjust a reward down when you use it. If you have a $4 +UP reward, you can't use it to buy a $3.99 item; you'll need to have something else in your order to get it over $4 in order to use it.

Rebates

Rite Aid also runs a Single Check Rebates (SCR) program, at riteaid1.rebateplus.com. This works a little differently in that you don't receive OYNO (on your next order) coupons at the register. Instead, you enter 3 digits off of each qualifying receipt online, then are able to request a lump sum rebate on a single check at the end of each month.

> **HEADS-UP**
>
> Once you request a Single Check Rebate (SCR) check, no more rebates will post for that month. Make sure you don't have any receipts that you have not yet entered before requesting.

As with any rebate, be sure to keep track of your receipts. Enter your purchases right away so you don't lose a receipt or forget to do so before the end of the month, when it expires.

Video Values

At Rite Aid's Video Values site (riteaid.adperk.com), watch advertising videos to access printable coupons and special offers. These change monthly, so check back at the beginning of the month for new videos and offers.

Coupon Limits

Rite Aid now limits customers to using four "like" manufacturer coupons per transaction. A like coupon is an identical coupon—same dollar amount, same expiration date.

Saving on Prescriptions

Whether you fill your prescriptions at drugstores or anywhere else, you'll be looking for ways to save. Even if you are covered by insurance, plans are getting skimpier and deductibles are rising. Here are a few ways to save at the drugstore and beyond.

Prescription Programs

See if your drugstores offer prescription savings programs, such as Rite Aid's free Rx Savings program (riteaid.com/pharmacy/rx_savings.jsf). Beware, though, of scam artists trying to sell fraudulent prescription drug or Medicare cards.

Manufacturer Offers

Whenever you're prescribed a new drug—particularly if it's a long-term maintenance prescription—check the manufacturer's website to see if they have any offers. Some provide coupons for a first month's supply, while others provide ongoing discounts. Pfizer, for example, provides a $4 co-pay card for its best-selling cholesterol-lowering drug, Lipitor (www.lipitor.com/patients/lipitorforyou.aspx), and Advair offers a first month's prescription free plus ongoing special offers when you sign up for their e-mail list (www.advair.com/asthma/coupons-and-special-offers/asthma-registration.html).

Prescription Coupons

You'll also want to keep your eye out for prescription coupons in store ads and online. These offer an incentive for filling a new prescription or transferring a prescription, often a $10 or $25 store gift card. Target often prints these in their Sunday ads, as does Kmart; both stores also sometimes post printable prescription coupons online. At grocery stores, prescription coupons can be found in in-store brochures or occasionally printed out as Catalinas.

HEADS-UP

Some drugstores and other pharmacies are placing new restrictions on these coupons. They're aware that some customers transfer the same prescription back and forth each month to continue receiving gift cards at each refill, so some pharmacies now only accept these types of coupons for prescriptions you've never filled before there. Others require you to wait three months between transfers before it's considered a "new" prescription again. Also, if you are taking a lot of different prescriptions, be aware that moving these between pharmacies can make it more difficult for pharmacists to notice potential drug interactions.

Some drugstores, such as CVS, also accept competitor pharmacy coupons. Check with yours for their policy. Prescription coupons can be a fantastic way to save—you have to fill the prescription anyway, so why not get some money back? Then, stretch that gift card as far as it can go by playing the money-back rewards game at your drugstore of choice.

Samples at the Doctor's Office

When your doctor writes any prescription, be sure to ask if their office has samples available. Pharmaceutical representatives often provide these for physicians to give out to their patients. In the case of a short-term antibiotic prescription, they might even have a sufficient supply right there so you don't have to fill it at all.

Warehouse Clubs

Prescription costs are often lower at warehouse clubs, and you don't need to be a member to use the pharmacy. Call around and compare costs before filling a prescription; in some cases you might save hundreds of dollars.

If it's more convenient for you to fill prescriptions at your local grocery store, some match pharmacy prices at local competitors. Ask your local store about its policy.

Generics

Generic drugs are generally lower-cost—often dramatically lower. Ask your physician if there's a generic alternative that might work just as well, since they don't always think to offer alternatives without being prompted.

Target offers hundreds of generic drugs at $4 for a 30-day supply, and $10 for a 90-day supply (sites.target.com/site/en/spot/page. jsp?title=pharmacy_generic_drugs_alphabetical). Walmart offers a similar $4/$10 program for generic prescription drugs plus some

over-the-counter medications; access their list at www.walmart.com/
cp/PI-4-Prescriptions/1078664. (Note that in some states prices may
be higher—check with your local pharmacy for details.)

Other pharmacies, such as Meijer and ShopRite, actually offer select
common antibiotics, and sometimes prenatal vitamins, for free.

The Least You Need to Know

- Walgreens has its own unique set of rules for its Catalina
  program, Register Rewards (RR).
- Rite Aid and CVS run their own money-back rewards programs.
  Roll these into new money-back items.
- Look for coupons and savings on prescriptions just as with
  groceries, toiletries, or anything else you buy.

Couponing Strategies

In This Chapter

- Good things come to those who wait: use high-value coupons during sales
- Smaller items often bring higher savings
- Save as many ways as possible on every item

Now that we've talked about the different types of coupons and some basic saving strategies, let's start putting all of these things together. You really save big at the store when you start shopping strategically, and this is where you'll start to see how to pick up items for free or pennies on the dollar, every single week.

This chapter outlines the best times to use your high-value coupons, how to shop strategically to best match up coupons with sales, and how to stack up multiple types of savings on a single item to get products for pennies on the dollar.

Patience Is a Virtue

When we see a high-value coupon for a product we like, whether in the newspaper, in the store, or online, our first impulse is to run out and use it right away. Why not, right? It's good to save! Smart couponers, though, bide their time and wait for the optimum time to use those high-value coupons. Here's why.

When you use a coupon on an item at its high everyday price at the store, your percentage of savings is generally very low. This is one of the reasons that people think they can't really save with coupons, because it's hard to see the savings when they're a drop in the bucket of your everyday spending.

However when you wait to use a coupon until an item goes on sale, your percentage of savings will be much, much higher. Stacking a coupon together with a sale price can often result in 50 percent—or more—savings, and sometimes even makes an item free.

There have been times when I have waited months to use a high-value coupon, although you'll want to watch those expiration dates. One August, for example, Libby's put out a newspaper coupon for $1 off three Libby's canned vegetables. Right off the bat, this is a pretty good coupon, because Libby's canned veggies aren't all that expensive to begin with; they run $1 a can or less at everyday prices.

But what happens when you wait? I'd picked up several papers that week, and had several coupons to use. I waited, and waited, and waited … until finally, in October, Dollar General put these vegetables on sale 3/$1! By simply waiting a couple of months to use these high-value coupons, I ended up with several month's worth of free canned veggies for my family by using a $1/3 coupon on a 3/$1 sale.

COUPON QUIPS

Savings add up, and pennies count. Just as your grocery bill climbs ever higher when you throw a little bit of this and a little bit of that into your cart, your savings climb ever higher when you're saving a few bucks on every single thing that you buy. A few bucks here, a few bucks there, and soon you're talking about hundreds of dollars of savings a month.

When you think about these savings individually, you might think: Well, so what? She saved a few bucks on canned veggies. But think about it this way: these savings are cumulative. I'm not just getting veggies for free—I'm also getting toothpaste for free and granola bars for free and crackers for free and shampoo for free.

When I can shop from my pantry for all of these items rather than spending money out of pocket to restock each week, it leaves extra money in my grocery budget for whole foods and my family's priorities.

Bigger Is Not Always Better

We're conditioned in this country to think that bigger is always better: the largest size is always the best deal, warehouse clubs are the way to go, buying in bulk saves you money. Coupons, though, turn that conventional wisdom on its head. When it comes to coupons, the smallest size—and sometimes even the trial or travel size!—is often the best deal.

Here's how the math works out, with a real life example. The other day, I was standing in my local grocery store looking at two packages of Bounty napkins. The 50-count pack sold for $1.25, while the 200-count pack sold for $3.50.

On the face of it, the 200-count pack is a better deal, right? To get 200 napkins in 50-count packs, I'd have to buy four for $5— so buying the bigger pack is $1.50 cheaper than buying four small packs.

But I was standing there holding a $1 off coupon for any size Bounty napkins from a recent newspaper insert. Using this coupon on the 50-count pack gets me 50 napkins for $.25. Using this coupon on the 200-count pack gets me 200 napkins for $2.50—the equivalent of $.625 for each pack of 50. I save more than twice as much by using this coupon on the smaller package, even though the bigger pack is a better purchase if you don't have the coupons.

This sort of thing happens all the time when you use coupons. Your initial per-unit cost is often smaller on the larger-size item; but since your percentage of savings is so much higher with coupons on the smaller item, this more than makes up for the difference. You can often purchase items very cheaply, sometimes even for free, by using higher-value coupons on smaller items.

With Store Coupons, Too

This type of savings on smaller items is possible with store coupons, too. Target, in particular, often releases printable store coupons that make smaller items free. Just tonight, for example, I picked up a 2-pack of Sharpies on a school supplies special for $1, used a $1 off any Sharpie product coupon from the Target website, and paid nothing for my markers. Last month, I used a $1 off any Up & Up (Target brand) pain relief item to pick up a $.99–20-count bottle of ibuprofen for free.

> **COUPON QUIPS**
>
> One perk of using store coupons to purchase items for free is that, since they come off as a store discount, they reduce the item's price to zero. This reduces your taxable amount to zero, even in states where you would have to pay the entire tax on your before–manufacturer coupon totals.

Buying Trial and Travel Items

Now, let's talk travel sizes. For the sake of our example here, let's say that you have a $1 off coupon for ANY size Tide detergent. (They really do put these in the Sunday coupon inserts on occasion.) Bottles of Tide sell for about $7, and go on sale as low as $5, on rare occasions.

Saving $1 off $7? That's all right I guess, but it's not a very high percentage of savings. What's better, though? If you have multiple coupons, why not buy several little travel-size Tides that sell for $.97 in the travel section, making them free after your $1-off-any-size coupon.

This is also a great plan for using coupons that would otherwise go to waste. Let's say you always buy Purex rather than Tide, because you can purchase it much more cheaply at your local store by combining coupons with sales. You're never likely to use a $1-off-Tide coupon on the big bottle, because you're stocked up on cheap Purex, and end up just throwing these coupons in the recycle bin.

Instead, why not pick up some free travel-size Tide next time you're at the store, just to supplement your stockpile of other brands? You've already bought the newspaper, and already have the coupon (or coupons!) in hand. The coupon doesn't go to waste, you score free items, and you won't run out of detergent when you quickly use up the tiny travel size—since you already have a stockpile of Purex at hand.

HEADS-UP

Pay attention to the wording on your coupons! If you start playing this trial-and-travel game, be sure always to read the fine print. You'll notice that some coupons specifically exclude trial or travel sizes, or will specify a certain size in ounces, while others will not; if your coupon specifically excludes the smaller size, save it for a sale on the larger version.

When you have high-value coupons without size restrictions, bring them along and take a stroll through the trial-and-travel section to see what you can see.

Using Trial and Travel Items

So what do you do with the free travel-size items you accumulate this way? Here are a few ideas:

- Travel with them! You'll never run out of 3-ounce containers for your 1-quart zip-top bags if you stockpile for your trips.

- Donate them! Homeless shelters, battered women's shelters, and more can make good use of these.

- Send them to the troops! These were great to send to my Army-boy brother when he was deployed overseas.

- Pretty up your guest bedroom and bathroom. Visitors might like their own little shampoos, lotions, soaps, and more.

- Refill your full-size bottles with the tiny ones you get for free.

- Use them. Travel-and-trial–size items are another great way to experiment and see which brands you like.

- Let the kids use them. Kids love tiny items, so let them use the ones that are appropriate for their age group.

As always, if you can't use these yourself, there's someone out there who can.

Stack Up Your Savings

Saving one time on one item is great. Saving two times on one item? Twice as good! To really save with coupons, you'll always want to be looking for ways to stack your savings. When you stack, you're layering different savings methods on top of each other for maximum impact.

The most basic example of stacking is what we've been talking about all along: using coupons on top of sale prices to maximize savings and start your stockpile. But let's start getting a little more tricky— and really start to save.

Stack Store and Manufacturer Coupons

Way back in Chapter 2, we talked about the differences between store and manufacturer coupons. The most important difference here is that manufacturer coupons are a form of payment for a product, while store coupons are one way for a store to put an item on sale.

Why is this important? Manufacturer and store coupons come out of two different pots—one is a payment from the manufacturer, one is a discount from the store. This means that you can use them *together* to double up your savings on a single item.

HEADS-UP

Never try to use two paper manufacturer coupons on a single item, even if their values are different. Since these both come out of the same pot, the manufacturer won't want to pay twice for one item.

Stacking store and manufacturer coupons together can result in amazing savings, often giving you items for free. Here are just a few of the free items I've picked up recently using this method:

- Walgreens—free PediaCare: using a $5 in-ad store coupon with a printable manufacturer $2 coupon.

- Walgreens—free Reach toothbrushes: using a $1 in-ad store coupon with a $1 manufacturer newspaper coupon.

- Target—free Aquafresh training toothbrushes: using a $1 printable Target coupon with a $1 manufacturer coupon.

- Dominick's (Safeway)—free Mission tortillas: using a $1 in-ad coupon with a $1 printable manufacturer coupon.

- CVS—free Revlon nail clippers: using a $2 coupon from the price scanner with a $2 manufacturer printable.

Just about every week, you can pick up one or more free items simply by stacking store and manufacturer coupons. Whenever you see a store coupon—whether in-ad, in store, or online—see if you can find a manufacturer coupon to match up with it.

Stack Paper and E-Coupons

This is one of those times where *your mileage may vary (YMMV)*. At some stores, the cash registers will allow you to stack paper manufacturer coupons together with e-coupons on sites like Cellfire. At other stores, the register will beep when they scan the paper coupon, and you'll have to choose which to use. Stores are moving toward not allowing the use of both, and it's likely that as registers are upgraded, this practice will eventually end.

 DEFINITION

When couponers say **your mileage may vary (YMMV),** they mean that people's experiences trying a deal will differ; what works for one person may not work for another. A paper coupon may stack with an e-coupon, or it may not. Upgraded registers in one store might kick out a coupon, while in other stores they'll go through. Some cashiers will push through a coupon over the price of an item, others will not. When a deal depends on outside factors, your mileage may vary.

On store e-coupon sites, are these manufacturer or store coupons? The confusing answer is: they can be either. Some stores are moving the store coupons you would normally find in your weekly ad online, to save customers time in clipping.

At some Safeway-affiliated chains for example, Just for U (JFU) contains all of the store coupons you would normally find in the weekly ad, as well as store coupons for Safeway-brand items, those you can also find in brochures in store, and other random store electronic coupons. (Click the "Just for U" link on your local store's website to find the right JFU site for your local Safeway chain.)

Just for U also contains hundreds of manufacturer coupons, which are often similar to the printable coupons you would find on Coupons.com or the electronic coupons customers at other stores can load at sites like Cellfire. Safeway does not let you stack a paper manufacturer coupon with an electronic manufacturer coupon you have loaded on Just for U; the register will beep and prompt you to choose which you'd like to use.

Unfortunately, there is currently no easy way to tell which are store coupons and which are manufacturer coupons on Just for U. So bring along your paper coupons, and take them back graciously if the register kicks them out.

Stack Coupons and Catalinas

In Chapter 6, we talked about Catalina coupons, particularly about the dollars-off-your-next-order (OYNO) coupons that sometimes print out when you buy qualifying items. At most stores, you need to hit the required dollar amount or number of items to generate a dollars-off-your-next-order Catalina *before* any coupons are scanned.

This is the best possible news for couponers. Remember, dollars-off-your-next-order Catalinas trigger either when you purchase a certain number of participating products (buy five, get $5 OYNO), or when you hit a certain dollar amount on participating products (buy $25, get $10 OYNO).

HEADS-UP

At some stores, while manufacturer coupons do not affect whether a Catalina prints, store coupons do. This is because store coupons are seen as giving a discounted price rather than as a form of payment for the item. When you discount the price with a store coupon, the register sees that you have spent less on the qualifying items, which can drop you under the necessary dollar amount.

Using our "buy $25 in participating products, get $10 back on your next shopping order" example: that makes your net cost on those items $15. Let's say you buy $25 worth of participating products, but use $10 in coupons on those products. Now you have only spent $15 out of pocket, but you are still getting back $10 to use on your next shopping trip, making your net cost for those items just $5.

$25.00 in participating products
-$10.00 in coupons
-$10.00 in an on-your-next-order Catalina
_____

$5.00—an 80 percent savings!

Often, participating items on Catalina deals are also on sale. This lets you stack a coupon, with a sale price, with a money-back OYNO offer. Saving three times on one item? Yes, please!

Stack Coupons and Drugstore Rewards

Back in Chapter 7, we talked about rewards programs at various drugstores. You can stack these money-back rewards with coupons just as with grocery store Catalinas—but let's go one better!

The three major drugstore chains—Walgreens, CVS, and Rite Aid—often have items in their ads that are *free* after rewards. Buy a bottle of Gillette body wash for $4, for instance, and get a $4 Register Reward at Walgreens.

What happens when you use a $1 off coupon on that same $4 item? Now you're paying $3 out of pocket for your item—and still getting $4 back on your next shopping order at Walgreens. In effect, it's almost like they are paying you to take that bottle of body wash out of the store. You're getting paid to shop!

Roll Your Catalinas and Rewards

What's the best use for that $4 Register Rewards you just earned? You could use it to buy whatever you want in the store. Or you could use it to buy something else that's also giving back Register Rewards! Using previously earned rewards to pay lets you continue to pick up items without spending much else out of pocket, getting these products at little or no cost to you.

Let's say you wait a week, and in the new ad see that Advil is now on sale for $4 with a $4 Register Reward. Use the $4 RR you earned from Gillette body wash to buy your Advil. Pay just tax (if OTC medications are taxable in your state), and get a shiny new $4 RR to use on something else.

Remember back in Chapter 5 when we talked about the cost of brand loyalty? This is where it really comes into play. Maybe Gillette isn't your favorite brand of body wash. But just maybe, it's a perfectly acceptable alternative if you're getting it essentially for free.

This system works at any drugstore chain. Each offers different free or cheap after-rewards items every week, so keep rolling your rewards to pick up different HBA (health-and-beauty aisle) items all the time. This is a major way you can get your toiletries for free, rather than using generics or picking them up at Target, Walmart, or warehouse clubs.

The Least You Need to Know

- The more ways you can stack your savings on one item, the bigger potential gain.
- Use coupons on smaller items to get them for pennies on the dollar—or for free!
- Good things come to those who wait. Bide your time and use high-value coupons when they'll have the most impact.
- Roll your rewards into items that give you new rewards to keep getting items cheap (or free) without spending real money.

Online and Mobile Couponing

Couponing isn't just for the grocery store any more. As more of our life and our purchases move online, you'll want to save on everything you do and buy there as well. We'll start with a whirlwind tour of cash-back sites that give you rebates for your regular online shopping. If you're making a purchase from an online retailer, why not get a percentage back? Also find out how to use in-store rebates for bonus savings, and how to combine these with coupons to actually get paid to buy products.

Then we talk about deal-of-the-day sites, but we won't stop with Groupon. Explore alternatives that might have better deals for yourself and your family, and find out ways to resell and buy vouchers on the daily deals aftermarket.

You have learned not to go to the grocery store without your coupons—now, never shop online without your coupon codes. Coupon codes give you a percent off, dollars off, or free shipping on your online purchases. And add mobile couponing to the mix; grab discounts in the store when you're out and about just by installing a few key apps on your smart phone.

Lastly, we'll talk Amazon—who has scads of hidden coupon codes and discounts for savvy shoppers. Find the sneaky codes on Amazon, and sneak yourself discounts elsewhere by grabbing discount gift cards, finding hidden codes, and online comparison shopping for a better deal.

Cash Back and Rebates

In This Chapter

- Get cash back for almost everything you buy online
- Load electronic coupons for additional cash back or college savings from physical stores
- Find rebates online for many of your in-store purchases

Another way to stack up savings is by adding cash back to your online and offline purchases. Get a percentage of your purchase price back on almost everything you buy online, and find mail-in rebates for your in-store items.

You'll also want to look into newer electronic coupon and college savings sites that work like rebates, giving you money back into an online account that you can later cash out.

This chapter explores the many ways we can get money back for everyday purchases. If you're buying something anyway, you might as well get the cash back for it!

Cash-Back Sites

Cash-back rebate sites give a percentage of your online purchases at various retailers' sites back to you. To use these, instead of starting directly at the website of your online retailer, you instead start at the cash-back site.

At any of these sites, you'll need first to create an account or login. Then browse by alphabetical categories, or search for a specific retailer, then click through to their site from the cash-back site.

The cash-back site will open up your retailer's site in a new window, track your visit, and give you a specified percentage of your purchases into your cash-back account. When you hit a certain amount in your cash-back account, usually $5 to $10, they'll send you a check, or deposit it into your PayPal account.

Note that funds have to be "available" rather than "pending" before you can request or receive payment. This often takes up to 90 days after they show up as pending in your cash-back account.

Be sure not to close the new window that opens up to your retailer, since you lose your cash-back tracking if you end the session. Every time you want to make a qualifying cash-back purchase, you need to click again through the cash-back site and shop from the window that opens up.

HEADS-UP

Completing a transaction ends the cash-back session; so if you want to buy another item, you'll need to close the window and click back through to open up a new session. Sessions do time out, so don't open a window in the morning, go out all day, then come back in the evening and complete the purchase. Do it as soon as possible after opening the cash-back session.

Other restrictions sometimes apply, for instance, certain items might not be eligible for cash-back. Be sure to read the details on the cash-back site for each retailer.

HEADS-UP

It does take time, sometimes even weeks after the item ships, for these rebates to post into your account. They want to make sure that you haven't canceled your order and that everything goes through smoothly. So don't panic if you don't see your cash back appear right away. (And if you do cancel an order, they will reverse your cash back.)

You'll want to sign up for more than one of these sites, as each contains a different mix of participating retailers, most offer a sign-up bonus, and you might get a higher rebate for a given retailer on one site than on another. Some also offer online coupon codes, so when you click through it automatically clips the coupon for you and gives you both the cash-back bonus and coupon discount. (You may have to paste the code at checkout; use Ctrl-V on a PC.)

Some sites also offer you cash back for referring your friends. If you share your personal referral link with friends via e-mail, Facebook, or Twitter, you'll get paid (usually around $5) for each one who signs up for and makes a purchase through that site. This payment deposits into your cash-back account.

Here are just a few popular cash-back sites that you might want to check out. You might settle on just two or three to use regularly.

Ebates

Ebates (ebates.com) is one of the biggest and oldest cash-back sites. They currently offer a $5 sign-up bonus (which goes right into your new cash-back account), and issue checks or pay via PayPal quarterly to all accounts containing over $5.01—but your sign-up and friend referral bonuses don't count toward the minimum. You can also choose to donate your cash back to charity, or send it to an organization or family member.

Ebates also runs regular double cash-back events, where retailers offer bonus cash back over their usual percentage. You'll also see holiday specials: Around Mother's Day, for instance, they'll offer bonus cash back on sites that sell flowers and chocolate. At Christmas, you'll see bonus cash back at toy and electronics sites. If you're planning on a non–time-sensitive purchase, wait for a bonus cash-back event to take advantage of the additional rebate.

Ebates will e-mail you almost daily with bonus cash-back offers and deals of the day, so be sure to use your non-primary e-mail account to sign up.

eBillme

eBillme (ebillme.com) offers a way to shop online without using a credit card. Instead, when you check out with eBillme, you pay your online shopping bills using your online banking. (You can also pay with cash by walking into places like MoneyGram, but this typically involves a $4.95 fee—don't do it!)

Beyond an alternative bill pay method, eBillme offers cash back when you: shop through their site, click through to participating retailers, checkout with eBillme, and pay using your bank's online bill pay. They often run a "2x Thursday," where you'll receive double the posted cash-back percentage.

> **COUPON QUIPS**
>
> Unlike most other cash-back sites, eBillme offers cash back for electronic gift card purchases—including for popular sites like Amazon.com. Electronic gift cards come via e-mail. You either print them out and use them at the store just like a plastic gift card, or get a code to redeem for credit at online retailers.

At eBillme, you can cash out when you hit $10 in your cash-back account. This works a little differently, though: You do not receive actual cash back. Instead, you get eBillme credit that you can turn into a cash-back coupon, redeemable at hundreds of participating online retailers. So if you cash out for a $10 cash-back coupon, you can use that as a $10 credit at any of their participating sites. (If you want instead to receive your rewards as cash, you'll need to hit $50 in your cash-back account.)

eBillme, unlike some other cash-back sites, also has limits on what you can earn—currently a maximum of $20 cash back on a single transaction, and $200 in a calendar year.

FatWallet

The popular FatWallet couponing site also runs a cash-back program (fatwallet.com/cash-back-shopping). Click on "Cash Back Sales" at top right to see a list of stores with increased cash-back bonuses today—sometimes up to double the regular percentage.

HEADS-UP

When browsing other areas of FatWallet, only links with the Cash Back logo qualify for cash back. Links in forums don't qualify—even if that retailer does participate in their cash-back program—you need to click through from the Cash Back Sales area of the site or from designated links.

At FatWallet, as soon as cash back posts to your account, you can request a check or PayPal payment. These are processed weekly.

Mr. Rebates

Like Ebates, Mr. Rebates (mrrebates.com) offers a $5 sign-up bonus. Once you reach $10 in your cash-back account, you can request payment via check or PayPal. Both check and PayPal payments are processed at the beginning of the calendar month, so if you request payment in July, you'll receive it in early August.

Cash-Back College Savings

Upromise (upromise.com) is the largest site that gives you cash back into college savings. Use your earnings on their site in various ways:

- Link a Sallie Mae loan and automatically transfer quarterly savings to help bring that down.

- Open a high-yield Sallie Mae savings account and have your earnings automatically deposit.

- Open or link a 529–college savings account, then have your earnings automatically transfer.

- Request a check (once quarterly) so that you can deposit earnings into your own account.

You'll need to have $10 in earnings before you can request a check or have these transfers go through.

Upromise allows you to designate anyone you want as your Upromise beneficiary. You can choose yourself (go back to school, pay off college loans), a child or children, a godchild, a niece, a friend—anyone.

HEADS-UP

Upromise continually tries to upsell site visitors with pop-ups, e-mails, and ads; they want you to install their toolbar, sign up for their credit card, and more. You do not have to take advantage of any of these additional offers to participate or to save for college.

You have many cash-back options with Upromise, and here are the main ways to save.

Online Cash Back

First, you can use Upromise in the same way as all the other cash-back sites: start your online shopping at Upromise, then click through from their site to various online retailers to get a percentage of your purchases back as college savings. When making an online purchase, decide before you click whether you want your money back as general cash back on a site (like Ebates), or cash-back college savings at a site (like Upromise).

Dining Out

Register your credit cards at Upromise, then enter your ZIP code in the "dining out" portion of their site to find participating restaurants and cash-back percentages. Use your registered credit cards to pay for your meal, and get a percentage of your restaurant dining back as college savings. Note that restrictions apply, and some restaurants only give cash back on week nights, so read the fine print.

Credit Card

Upromise offers its own cash-back credit card through Bank of America. Their card gives 1 percent back on general purchases, 10 percent cash back on participating drugstore items, 2 percent back on fuel at ExxonMobil, and 2 percent bonus cash back when you use it to pay for online purchases made through Upromise.

Cash-Back E-Coupon Programs

Newer types of electronic coupon programs work less like e-coupons than like rebates at grocery stores and drugstores. Savings don't come off at the register, but you get the cash back later. The largest of these, SavingStar, grew out of the Upromise electronic college savings program but has now spun off into its own site.

At SavingStar (savingstar.com), as with other major e-coupon sites, you create an account, put in your ZIP code to see which stores participate in your area, and register your loyalty cards. In addition to grocery stores, SavingStar also partners with drugstores like CVS that have a loyalty card program.

As you browse the list of available e-coupons, click "I want this!" under each one that you want loaded to your card(s). A new batch of SavingStar e-coupons becomes available at the beginning of each month, and they also occasionally add a few new ones throughout the month.

When you purchase a qualifying product, your SavingStar e-coupon does not come off at the register like a regular electronic coupon does. Instead, the savings are deposited into your SavingStar account. Once you hit $5 in that account, you can cash out via direct deposit, PayPal, or for an Amazon gift card—or, you can donate your savings to charity. Note that it sometimes takes several weeks before you'll see your purchase credited into your account, so don't panic if you don't see it there right away.

Online Rebates for In-Store Purchases

You can also find mail-in rebate offers online for items you purchase in brick-and-mortar stores. Some of these offer the full purchase price back; others offer a set dollar amount.

> **TIPS AND TRICKS**
>
> You'll find several types of rebates: Mail-in rebates (MIR) offer back your entire or partial purchase price, or let you send in for a gift or coupons with proof of purchase. Try-me-free (TMF) rebates are generally for new products, and offer the entire purchase price back to entice you to try something new. Satisfaction guarantees send your money back if you don't like a product. Note that satisfaction guarantees are meant for people who are dissatisfied with the product; it's good couponing ethics not to send these in just to get money back on products you actually like.

You have two great ways to begin finding rebate forms and offers. First, check the manufacturer's website. While you're there looking for coupons, also look for rebate offers.

Secondly, take a look at Couponing to Disney's rebate database (couponingtodisney.com/earn-cash/rebates). You can click on any rebate she has listed to see more details and print the necessary form.

Also keep an eye out for rebate forms whenever you're walking through a store. Sometimes these are found on tearpads near the product, or are actually taped onto the product itself.

Track Rebates Online

Some sites also allow you to track the status of your rebates online to see if they have been mailed, or if they have been received and are pending. Check the status of rebates mailed to El Paso, Texas, at Web-Rebates.com, and check many other rebates at RewardsByMail. com.

Stack with Coupons

Most mail-in rebates give you the full precoupon purchase price of the item back! This means that you can actually make money by sending in for rebates, although you'll have to account for the cost of your stamp and your time.

> **HEADS-UP**
>
> Sometimes you'll see silly little rebate forms for, say, $1 back on a given item. After the cost of your stamp, you've only made a whopping $.56! Some people don't bother to send in for rebates under $5 because of the time it takes to fill out the forms and collect UPCs and receipts. As always, only you know what your own time is worth.

Check the wording on your rebate form to see if it mentions anything about coupons. Some of the forms found next to a coupon for the same product in the Sunday inserts, for instance, automatically deduct the amount of that coupon from your rebate.

If they don't, though, rebates are gravy. Let's say you find a mail-in rebate in-store for the full purchase price of a box of Kellogg's Fiber Plus granola bars. You have a coupon from the Sunday newspaper inserts for $.75 off a box of Kellogg's Fiber Plus granola bars. Buy the product, use your coupon, and you've covered the cost of your stamp—plus a tiny bit extra. The higher value coupon you have, the more money you'll make.

Stack with Money-Back Rewards

Even better: stack your rebates with money-back rewards at the grocery and drugstore. Let's say your Kellogg's Fiber Plus granola bars are on sale for $3.50 at your local store—but you get back a $1 Catalina coupon good toward your next shopping order when you buy one box, and you're still clutching that $.75 off coupon.

$3.50 Fiber Plus bars
-$.75 coupon
-$1.00 Catalina
-$3.50 rebate
_____
-$1.75

You just made $1.75 by buying a box of granola bars! You will have to subtract $.44 for your first-class stamp, so after that you're only up $1.31. But think about it: you just made money by buying granola bars. The item wasn't just free—you are getting paid to take it out of the store.

This is just a small example, too. With higher-value coupons and Catalinas, you can end up much further ahead.

Cash-Back Credit Cards

For most online purchases, you need to use a credit card. Most cards offer about 1 percent cash back, with additional bonuses on specific categories or during promotional periods.

TIPS AND TRICKS

Stack those savings yet again: Use a cash-back credit card on top of a cash-back rebate site, and get paid back twice for the same purchase. Use a cash-back credit card at the grocery store, and get money back on the portion you're not covering with coupons. Use a cash-back credit card at a participating Upromise restaurant, and get paid back twice for dining out.

Some credit cards offer cash-back bonuses at particular sites, such as the Amazon Visa card, which offers triple points for purchases made at Amazon. Others offer rewards at specific brick-and-mortar locations, such as the ExxonMobil MasterCard, which gives rebates on gas, or the Target REDcard, which gives 5 percent off all Target purchases.

Think about your shopping patterns when deciding which card or cards to sign up for. Track your purchases, and only buy items with your cards that you have the cash to pay off.

Don't Buy Just to Buy

As with the cash-back rebate sites, never, ever, buy a product just to get cash back on your credit card. If you're already purchasing them, however, you might as well use a card that's going to give you cash back—as long as you're paying off that card every month.

Quarterly Specials

Many credit cards, such as Discover and Chase Freedom credit card, offer quarterly 5 percent cash back for bonus categories. You'll need to log in to your account and sign up for these quarterly offers; you don't automatically receive the extra cash back. They might, for example, give 5 percent back on grocery purchases one quarter, 5 percent on dining the next, 5 percent on fuel the quarter after. Make a note to sign up for these special bonuses at the beginning of each quarter.

Cash In for Noncash

Some cards let you cash in your points for gift cards, and often offer a bonus for doing so. Discover, for instance, lets you purchase $50 gift cards to restaurants, gas stations, and more for $45 in earned points. The Amazon Visa card lets you use your points for Amazon purchases; this now shows up as an option at checkout.

The Least You Need to Know

- Always click through cash-back sites when shopping online to get something back for your purchases.
- Stack up your savings by paying with cash-back credit cards.
- Rebates on in-store purchases can let you try items for free— or even make money on the deal.

Daily Deals

In This Chapter

- Daily deal sites and what you can find there
- Sign up for multiple sites to expand your options
- Share with friends for bonuses and freebies
- Look into resellers for missed deals or buyer's remorse

You've probably already heard of Groupon—but have you used LivingSocial, FamilyFinds, Eversave, BuyWithMe, or any of the other competing deal-of-the-day sites that have cropped up, seemingly overnight? The more daily deal options you have, the more likely you are to find the right ones for you.

In this chapter, find out about some of the best places to sign up for daily deal alerts, and find out why it's good to move beyond Groupon and expand your deal-of-the-day palate.

Deal-of-the-Day Sites

Each deal-of-the-day site works basically the same way. Visit the site to sign up for morning daily deal e-mails that notify you of each day's offerings. On some sites, you'll have the option of choosing Twitter and Facebook notifications, and some also offer mobile apps that let you view and purchase deals on the go. When you receive these daily notifications, click through to the site and choose the offers you'd like to buy before they sell out or expire.

Most deals last a day or less, although sometimes these sites run select deals for as long as a week, or until they sell out. Hot daily deals have been known to sell out in a matter of hours—and sometimes, in the case of airline promos and other popular limited availability items, within minutes.

Many sites require a certain number of vouchers to be purchased before your deal is guaranteed, but the growing popularity of daily deals makes it almost certain that they'll always reach that tipping point on the major sites.

> **HEADS-UP**
>
> Deal-of-the-day sites work hard to create an artificial sense of scarcity and urgency, telling us we'll miss out if we don't get in on a deal right this very second. It's not really a deal, though, if it's something your family neither uses nor needs. Only buy the deals that are right for you, and be very selective on what you purchase. Deals tend to repeat across sites, so you don't necessarily miss out if you don't buy right away.

Make checking your daily deals e-mails part of your morning routine over coffee. It's useful to have an idea ahead of time of what kind of deals you're looking for (such as restaurants, children's play places, or keratin treatments) and what you're willing to pay ($40 for a massage, $25 for a 5-punch pass), so when one pops up you're mentally prepared and ready to go.

There Can Be More Than One

You'll want to sign up for more than one daily deals site. Although Groupon has brand-name recognition, other sites sometimes run better discounts, have different offers, or may have great deals on smaller local restaurants, attractions, and services that can't afford Groupon's rates. Some also offer daily deals on actual products, rather than on services and dining, so you'll want to find the right mix for you.

If you're in a rural area or far from a major city, you'll find that daily deals sites offer fewer discounts on local businesses near you. These sites depend on group buying power, so generally start in large metropolitan areas and spread outward.

You can, however, take advantage of online deals, product discounts, and deals that are good at national chains, so don't give up hope. You can buy deals on AMC movie tickets or Old Navy or Vistaprint.com, no matter where you happen to live. Although you might not sign up for e-mails from sites that don't offer nearby local deals, deal blogs and other sites (see more in Chapter 15) always announce major national deals.

Another reason to sign up for multiple daily deals sites: many offer a $3–$10 sign-up credit for new users. This can be large enough to snag you a deal for free, so you might as well take advantage more than once. As always, use your separate e-mail account to sign up for these sites to keep your real e-mail box from overflowing with daily e-mails. If you find that a given site never seems to have deals that meet your needs, you can always unsubscribe.

Some sites also now let you sign in with Facebook Connect, which is a useful way to register for multiple sites using your Facebook account without having to remember multiple logins and passwords. You'll see a "Sign in with Facebook Connect" logo on the top right if this option is available.

If you have a dummy account that you keep separate from your real interactions with your Facebook friends, you might want to use that here as well. Note that Facebook Connect can give permission to companies to post on your Wall, send you e-mail, and more. When you sign up using Facebook Connect, it will tell you what permissions you are granting.

TIPS AND TRICKS

You don't want to get carried away and spam your friends, but most daily deals sites do offer you credits of $3–$10 for each new friend you refer who ends up making a purchase. Each provides handy links under your account to share the site via e-mail, Facebook, or Twitter. After you purchase a deal, they'll also generally invite you to share that great deal with your friends and provide a personal link or easy way to post or e-mail that deal. Use this sparingly to avoid annoying your friends.

In the following sections, find information on some of the major deal-of-the-day sites among the hundreds that have cropped up in Groupon's wake. These are just select examples; you might find that other sites are more useful for your needs or have better deals in your local area.

1SaleADay

1SaleADay (1saleaday.com) offers one deeply discounted product each day in five categories: 1SaleADay Main, Wireless, Family, Watch, and Jewelry. Their discounts are often on the order of 75 to 90 percent off list price, but be sure to read item descriptions thoroughly—especially on technology items, which might be several versions older than the current offerings, and are often refurbished.

1SaleADay also often offers free products with free shipping to customers who post a testimonial on their Facebook page or Twitter account. These randomly go live at midnight Eastern, and are generally sold out by fairly early in the morning. They also offer a "Chunk of Junk" sale a few times a year, where for $5 plus shipping you get a grab bag box of items randomly selected from previous deals. (These generally sell out in just a few minutes.) Lastly, they run periodic "sell-offs," where deals change over every half-hour all day.

BuyWithMe

BuyWithMe (www.buywithme.com) offers a different "BuyWithThree" twist: Purchase one of their deals of the day, and they'll give you a special referral link to share on Facebook, Twitter, and in e-mail. If three of your friends buy that very same deal through your personal link, your own deal is free. You can track which of your friends have purchased the deal, and they'll refund your purchase price within seven days if you earn yours for free from your friends' purchases.

BuyWithMe also keeps its offers live for seven days, or until they sell out, unlike single-day deals on most other sites.

Eversave

Eversave (www.eversave.com) offers both local and online saves, and often releases promo codes for $2 or $3 off of their deals. (These can be found on the site or in your daily e-mail, when available.) While Eversave started in just a few cities, they've been expanding quickly, and are worth keeping an eye on.

FamilyFinds

FamilyFinds (www.familyfinds.com) focuses its deals on both local and online products and services that appeal to families and children. Watch FamilyFinds specifically for deals at local family-friendly attractions and restaurants that you might not see at larger and less family-focused sites.

HEADS-UP

Some sites tend to list their family-oriented deals as side offers, so if you're in the market, always look beyond the main deal and at additional offerings on the site.

FamilyFinds also has a "suggest a deal" option, so it's worth putting in a plug for your favorite local restaurant, business, or attraction. If enough people ask for a given deal, it gives FamilyFinds an incentive to approach that business.

Groupon

Groupon (www.groupon.com), the site that started it all, now contains so many offers that you don't see all of them in your morning e-mail. Instead, it shows you the closest or most popular offer, and you need to click over to the site to see side or nearby deals. Sometimes the side deals can be much more interesting or pertinent for you, so try to remember to look beyond the main deal they're advertising.

Groupon has recently branched out into additional offerings, including Groupon Now and Groupon Getaways. Groupon Now (www. groupon.com/now), currently available in just a few cities, lets you enter your ZIP code to find nearby local deals to purchase for use that day—some have to be used within a matter of hours! Their offers range from restaurants to entertainment. If you don't use a Groupon Now buy, they'll automatically refund your purchase price.

Groupon Getaways (www.groupon.com/getaways) offers travel deals, such as discount hotel vouchers. You can sign up for Groupon Getaway alerts, which come in a separate e-mail from your general Groupon daily deals.

LivingSocial

LivingSocial (livingsocial.com) has a similar structure to BuyWithMe: If you get three friends to buy a deal you have purchased, you get yours for free. They don't charge your credit card until the next day to give a chance for you to earn a free deal.

Unlike BuyWithMe, LivingSocial deals are generally only live for one day (with some exceptions). They also offer a wider variety of deals, sometimes six or seven options within one geographical area, as well as a special section for family deals. LivingSocial also sometimes offers LivingSocial Escapes, or deep discounts to popular travel destinations like Jamaica or all-inclusive resorts in Mexico. Check their left sidebar for escapes, family, and adventure deals.

LivingSocial offers deals at local businesses plus online deals. As with Groupon, you can scroll down to see the additional deals that are available beyond the main deal they e-mail you; in some large urban areas they've also branched out into offering geographically targeted deals for suburbs. (West Suburban, Northwest Suburban, etc.)

MYHABIT

Amazon couldn't let the daily deal craze pass them by, so in spring 2011 they started their own limited-time-deals site at MYHABIT (www.myhabit.com). MYHABIT offers very limited quantities of deep-discount designer clothing and accessories each day, and these go live at 11 A.M. Central time. When they're gone, they're gone— and sometimes they sell out in a matter of minutes.

TIPS AND TRICKS

MYHABIT offers free shipping and free returns, so if an item doesn't fit you can return it on Amazon's dime for site credit.

On MYHABIT, you can sign in and pay using your Amazon account, and all of your Amazon gift cards or credits transfer over for use there as well. Amazon has offered occasional discount codes for MYHABIT, sometimes steep enough to make items free for those lucky enough to get in on the sales.

Target

Target offers several online daily deals each day (dailydeals.target. com), and daily Target deals always ship for free. You'll see one main deal, then scroll down for several others under their highlighted offer. These deals are often 50 to 60 percent off regular price, and range from clothes to toys to video game hardware.

Woot!

Woot! (www.woot.com) has been around for longer than most of the other daily deals sites. They offer one product deal per day, and you can generally buy up to three of the same item for the same flat $5 shipping fee. These are often refurbished technology items or appliances (Android tablets, Dyson vacuums), but their charm lies in their randomness. Check the right sidebar for links to associated deal sites kids.woot.com, wine.woot.com, shirt.woot.com, and deals.woot.com/ sellout.

Woot! also occasionally runs what they call a "Woot-off," in which limited quantity deals change over all day long as each item sells out. If you visit Woot.com and see spinning lights and a slider bar counting down the items remaining, you'll know to keep checking back in or refreshing the page (Ctrl-R on a PC) to see the new deals.

Local Daily Deals Sites

Local daily deals sites focus on a single city or suburban area, rather than offering national deals or deals across multiple cities like the major sites do.

HEADS-UP

Be careful when purchasing from newer local or smaller sites. Some end up not being able to hack the competition, and close up shop with no warning. When you buy a daily deal from a newer site, it's a good idea to print and redeem it as soon as possible.

Some of the longer-running and more stable sites are maintained by news or radio stations. CBS, for example, runs "CBS local" offers (offers.cbslocal.com) that automatically shows you local deals based on the IP address you log in from; you can switch cities using the Other Locations option at the top right of the screen.

Another example of a long-running local site is the Radio Shopping Show (www.radioshoppingshow.com), which currently airs in Las Vegas, Nevada, as well as Aurora and Elgin, Illinois. Sign up on their site for a free Money Saver key tag with a unique member number, then call in during the show and use that number to purchase everything from products, to discount certificates for local businesses or restaurants. A number of limited-time certificates are also available for purchase straight from their website.

Use Them or Lose Them

After you purchase a deal of the day, most sites e-mail you when your voucher is available. This is usually the same or next business day. At each of these sites, you can also access your current vouchers and print them out, or find your online code, under your account details; you can also mark each voucher as used after you have used them.

Many sites also e-mail you a reminder when your vouchers are close to expiration. You will want to print these out when you receive them and keep them in a folder or otherwise easily accessible, so you don't forget to use them.

While you generally won't lose the money you have put in, vouchers' additional value does expire. What does this mean? Let's say you purchase a $50 voucher to a local restaurant for $25. After the expiration date, that voucher will only be worth the initial $25 you paid for it; you'll lose all of the bonus value.

When you buy a deal, be sure you'll be able to use it before the stated expiration date.

HEADS-UP

You generally have to use the entire voucher amount in one visit or in one transaction; you can't, say, buy a $50 restaurant voucher and use $20 on one visit and $30 on the next.

If you find yourself unable to use a voucher or wish you hadn't made the purchase, you do have options. Most vouchers are transferable, unless prohibited by the original terms of the deal. Some people resell vouchers on eBay or Craigslist, but you can also look into sites specifically devoted to buying and selling daily deal vouchers.

Deal-of-the-Day Resellers

So let's say you buy a deal of the day and then have buyer's remorse. Or you never get around to using it, and then realize it's about to expire. You can try reselling your deal voucher on Craigslist or eBay, but might do better with sites specifically devoted to reselling and purchasing past daily deals.

Some sites charge a transaction fee for this service and actually facilitate the sale, while others serve as more of a listing service and are free for both buyers and sellers to use. Those that charge offer some protection to buyers, while at those that don't, you buy at your own risk.

Beyond selling your own vouchers, these are great places to look if you missed a deal and think later that you really should have picked it up. Just see if someone else is reselling theirs!

CityPockets

CityPockets (www.citypockets.com) offers a handy service to organize your daily deals: Sign up to import all of your daily deal vouchers from other sites into their site. You then have just one spot to check, and they'll e-mail you reminders before each is about to expire. CityPockets also provides a mobile app to let you track your deals while out and about, and you can redeem many of them right off your smartphone screen.

In addition to the organizational feature, CityPockets also lets you buy and sell past deals in their Marketplace (www.citypockets.com/marketplace). You need a PayPal account to buy or sell vouchers.

 HEADS-UP

You need to set up a PayPal account (www.paypal.com) to buy and sell at many sites, including eBay. PayPal allows you to buy and sell items online without exposing your credit card information.

If you wish to sell a voucher, you're free to set your own sale price, and CityPockets charges no listing fees. When your voucher sells, they charge sellers a transaction fee of $1, plus 8 percent of the sale price of the voucher. They'll deposit the sale price minus fees into your PayPal account.

CityPockets offers a buyer protection guarantee where they refund your purchase price if it turns out a seller has already used the deal or otherwise sells you an unusable voucher. Since CityPockets imports daily deals from sellers' accounts, in most cases they can guarantee that the deal is unused and still valid.

If you wish to buy a voucher, simply search or browse by category in your local area. When you purchase a voucher from a seller on CityPockets, it transfers immediately from the seller's MyVouchers page to your own MyVouchers page on CityPockets. You can then print and use it immediately.

CoupRecoup

CoupRecoup (couprecoup.com) is free to both buyers and sellers, and serves as a straight listing service rather than actually facilitating transactions like CityPockets does. When you go to CoupRecoup, it recognizes the city you're logging in from and automatically shows you the newest deal listings from sellers. You can change cities on the upper-right part of the screen or simply browse the available vouchers.

HEADS-UP

Since CoupRecoup merely facilitates the connection of buyers and sellers, it lacks the buyer protections of a site like CityPockets. Since it doesn't charge fees, sellers may charge a lower price for their vouchers.

To buy a deal, click the "contact seller" link to the right of each listing and enter your e-mail address and a note to the seller. You can either accept the seller's price, or in some cases make them an offer for their voucher. The seller receives your message in an e-mail and then is able to contact you to arrange the sale and transfer via whatever method works for you both.

DealsGoRound

Like CityPockets, DealsGoRound (www.dealsgoround.com) serves as both a way to organize all your daily deals purchases (via their "Deal Wallet") and as a site where you can buy and sell daily deals vouchers via PayPal. DealsGoRound currently operates in 128 U.S. and Canadian cities, and charges the seller a transaction fee of 10 percent of the selling price on each voucher sold.

On DealsGoRound, you can also post a wanted ad asking if anyone has a specific past deal from a specific daily deals site to sell, as well as sign up for weekly e-mails of new deals for sale in your city. If you have a deal to sell, you can post it online or browse wanted ads to see if anyone is looking for that particular deal.

DealsGoRound offers buyers a 60-day guarantee on vouchers sold through its site (as long as they haven't expired), and you can download their app for both iPhone and Android to keep track of deals and buy and sell deals on the go.

The Least You Need to Know

- Daily deals sites offer limited-time dramatic discounts of randomness.
- Don't forget to use these—they do expire.
- Before buying, be sure it's something your family really wants or needs.
- Buy and sell vouchers at reseller sites if you have regrets about a purchase or a missed opportunity.

In This Chapter

- Save money on dining out with codes, coupons, and gift certificates
- Sign up for restaurant birthday freebies
- Stack up the savings on dining out

Restaurants are a popular daily deals category, but you'll also want to take advantage of other places to pick up dramatically discounted restaurant vouchers and coupons, as well as online coupon codes for dining out.

While we want to save at the store and on all the meals we prepare at home, sometimes we'll also want to eat out. Here, find ways to save whenever you dine out.

Online Savings on Dining Out

While simply eating at home rather than dining out is the best way to save on meals, sometimes you just want someone else to do the cooking. Just as when you go to the grocery store, you'll want to maximize your savings whenever you go to a restaurant.

As we talked about in the previous chapter, deal-of-the-day sites are a wonderful way to save on dining out, often offering discount vouchers to local restaurants at 50 percent off or more. These are hit or miss, though—you have to choose from the random offers you find each day, so you can't just pick a favorite restaurant.

Luckily, you can find a number of other restaurant coupons, codes, and deals online that let you choose your preferred restaurant and provide more options for saving.

Restaurant.com

Restaurant.com sells discount gift certificates to local restaurants; just put in your ZIP code to see what's available in your area. These offers reset the first of every month, and popular restaurants do sell out fairly quickly.

Restaurant.com gift certificates vary in price depending on the popularity of the restaurant and what deal they choose to offer. Some $25 gift certificates sell for as low as $10, others for as high as $20.

Never pay even the regular Restaurant.com discounted price for these certificates. They always have a coupon code available, ranging from 40 percent off at the beginning of the month to as much as 80 percent off toward the end when they want to clear out their excess inventory. Find the current coupon code at sites like RetailMeNot.com, which we'll talk about in Chapter 13.

Restaurant.com certificates actually work much more like coupons than gift certificates. They generally have a minimum purchase requirement, often are not good on alcohol, are usually for dine-in only, and other restrictions sometimes apply. Be sure to read the fine print on every certificate before you buy to be sure it's still a good deal for you—even after the requirements.

TIPS AND TRICKS

Since popular restaurants sell out quickly on Restaurant.com, one strategy is to purchase a general gift certificate to Restaurant.com itself when the 80 percent discount codes come out toward the end of the month. Then, use that general gift certificate to buy certificates to "hot" restaurants when they reset at the beginning of the month, effectively giving yourself that deep discount then.

Whenever you buy a Restaurant.com gift certificate, go through a cash-back site like Ebates. You can generally get 15 percent cash back—sometimes higher. Restaurant.com is exceptionally generous on these sites, and you can generally get 24 percent cash back—and as high as 50 percent cash back on the occasional special event.

Just like when you shop at grocery stores or drugstores, always stack those savings. Combining a discount code, with cash back, with discount gift certificates lets you dine out for less. (Then pay the rest of your bill with a credit card that gives you cash back!)

Upromise

We talked about Upromise college savings in Chapter 9, but Upromise is also a great way to get cash back for dining. You'll first need to register your credit card at Upromise.com. Then, use that card when you dine at participating local restaurants to get a percentage of your purchase back into your Upromise account.

As with Restaurant.com, watch the restrictions on these. Put in your ZIP code on the Upromise site to see what restaurants participate in your area and what percent cash back you'll receive. Many restaurants only give cash back on weeknights, or have other exclusions, which are specified in their Upromise listings.

HEADS-UP

When deciding which credit cards to register and use with Upromise Dining, pick the ones that give you the highest cash back. Then, when you dine out, choose the card to pay with based on current specials. If Discover is running a bonus cash-back restaurant special this quarter, use Discover; if Chase Freedom is doing a restaurant bonus, use Chase.

Upromise also runs regular dining specials where you can earn bonuses by dining at participating restaurants a certain number of times in a given month. They'll e-mail members invitations to these promos, and you'll need to sign up to participate. Always sign up for their bonus offers; it costs you nothing, and even if you don't get the bonus, you lose nothing.

Birthday Clubs

These aren't just for kids anymore! Although you'll want to sign up your kids and your significant other, too—who wouldn't want a free ice cream cone from Baskin Robbins on their birthday, for instance? Many restaurants, ranging from Benihana to Noodles & Company, give you a coupon for a free meal in your birthday month. Dine out all month long on your savings. (And pick it up to go if you want to avoid all the extra expenses that come with a free meal!)

Some restaurants call these birthday clubs, while some just call them e-clubs or e-mail clubs. Either way, sign up for as many as possible. Start with your favorite local restaurants (check their websites for birthday club or e-club links) and branch out from there.

You can also use sites like FreeBirthdayStuff.com to find extensive lists of restaurants and other retailers that offer birthday freebies. (You'll have to sign up to access the full lists, but membership is free.)

TIPS AND TRICKS

Use your alternate e-mail address to sign up for restaurant birthday and e-clubs, because they'll advertise to you all year long.

Some chain restaurants, like Chili's and T.G.I. Friday's, also give you freebies just for signing up, such as a free appetizer or dessert. Others offer a free meal or dessert on your wedding anniversary or anniversary of joining their club, as well as random printable coupons throughout the year. Some—like Dairy Queen and Auntie Anne's pretzels—send out monthly coupons, while others run seasonal promotions.

National chains are more likely to offer e-mail clubs, although you'll want to check the websites of your favorite local joints as well.

Local Restaurant Coupons

You know those free coupon fliers and magazines that come in the mail? Don't throw them away without browsing, since they often contain great coupons for local restaurants. But you can also go online to print more. Check out:

- Clipper Magazine (CouponClipper.com)—Search, browse by category, read your local magazine, and sign up for daily deals.

- Money Mailer (www.moneymailer.com)—Print local coupons, download their iPhone app, and sign up for SMS (text message) coupons.

- ValPak (www.valpak.com)—Print coupons for local restaurants and businesses, plus sign up to receive deals via text messaging.

In some cities and large suburban areas you can find local coupon sites that contain coupons and discounts for only local businesses and restaurants. Start by typing "[*the name of your town*] coupons" on Google, and see what you can find.

COUPON QUIPS

When using any restaurant coupon or voucher, be sure to tip on the before-coupon amount. Don't penalize your server because you're getting a great deal.

Local coupon sites often contain restaurant coupons you don't find on the larger national sites, and might offer higher discounts for specific local restaurants or franchises. (One Subway restaurant, for example, might run a promo that's only good at their specific location, rather than at all Subways.) When using coupons from local sites or mailed magazines, read the fine print to see what locations are participating.

Restaurant Websites

Just as you visit manufacturer websites to find printable coupons for their products, check restaurant websites before you dine out. Both local restaurants and national chains often have printable coupons available on their websites, so take a minute to check before you go. Again, couponing doesn't have to take a lot of time—if you can spend a minute to save $5 or more, why not?

Bookmark the sites of your favorite local restaurants for easy clicking. Read the fine print or check that your location will accept a coupon before you order. These are often only good at participating locations, and independent franchises sometimes choose not to participate.

Read the Reviews

When you're thinking about trying a new place with a coupon or deciding whether to buy a voucher, customer reviews can be invaluable. Check sites like …

- Trip Advisor (www.tripadvisor.com)—even if you're not going on a trip, you can use it for restaurant reviews in your local area.

- Urban Spoon (www.urbanspoon.com)—the site and its associated app offer reviews and let you know how pricey a place is.

- Yelp (www.yelp.com)—search for a type of cuisine near your city and state, read reviews, and see average prices.

If you're out late or dressed casually and looking for a last-minute restaurant, these sites provide everything from hours, to dress codes, to average price range at restaurants in the ZIP code you enter.

The Least You Need to Know

- Use coupons, vouchers, or gift certificates whenever you dine out—save even when you splurge.
- Sign up for birthday clubs and restaurant sites to receive freebies and coupons via e-mail.
- Always try to "stack" your dining discounts—save twice or more on one meal!

Mobile Coupon and Savings Apps

Chapter 12

In This Chapter

- Mobile coupons for savings at the register
- Mobile apps for discounts and rewards
- Texting for coupons and freebies
- The privacy concerns of giving up information for discounts

In this chapter, we'll talk about how mobile apps and SMS alerts work to give you extra savings at the register. Plus, you'll see how to text for freebies and high-value coupons—right from your phone! From grocery coupon and planning apps to retail store rewards apps, there's an application out there for everyone.

You will need a smartphone to take advantage of apps and mobile sites, although you can do some of the SMS offers from any text-capable phone. Most apps are available for both iPhone and Android users, but you'll have fewer options if you have a BlackBerry.

Mobile Coupons

Even newer than electronic coupons, mobile coupons come in a variety of formats: SMS (text message), web, or through either store-specific or general coupon apps. These display on your phone, print from your phone, or provide you with codes you can use to receive your discount.

Some of the electronic coupon sites we talked about in Chapter 2 have associated mobile apps that allow you to "clip" your e-coupons while you're out and about, if you forget to do so before you go to the store. If you visit Cellfire.com on your mobile browser, for instance, they'll prompt you to download the Cellfire mobile app instead of viewing the regular Cellfire website.

Cellfire also provides some non-grocery retail coupons that you can access via your mobile phone. These give your cashier a code to type in to redeem that coupon at the register.

Similarly, Zavers has a mobile website where you can find e-coupons, and also allows you to load select coupons via SMS shortcodes (texting a short number to Zavers to automatically load coupons). Check the e-coupon site for your local grocery stores to see what apps are available.

Be sure also to check printable coupon sites to see if they have associated apps. Coupons.com, for instance, has its own mobile app, which allows you to print another set of coupons right from your phone (if you have a select supported printer!) and to see what coupons might be available while you are out and about.

SMS (Text) Coupons

Several major chains have been experimenting with mobile coupon delivery via text message. Some offer ongoing SMS promos, while others run occasional one-shot text offers. The Gap, for example, has run promos such as "text this number today only for your $25/$50 coupon!" They announce these types of promos on their Facebook page, in e-mails to registered customers, or on in-store signage.

HEADS-UP

Before signing up for any ongoing mobile coupon program that uses SMS, be sure you know what kind of monthly texting plan you have on your phone. Some freebies and coupon offers require multiple back-and-forth texts to verify your address information. If you're paying $.20 per text, those charges start eating up your coupon savings pretty quickly.

Here are just a few examples of store-specific SMS programs. Be sure to visit the websites of your favorite local stores or look for in-store signage about SMS clubs and promos.

While some of these mobile programs offer coupons and codes via text, others require users to receive the text and then load a mobile web page of coupons via their smartphone, while others send text alerts of the new offers and then require you to go online to clip the actual coupons and load them onto your loyalty card. Check out how each of these works if you don't have a web-capable phone; sometimes texting alone is not enough.

Meijer mPerks

At Meijer, create an account using your cellphone number at mPerks (www2.meijer.com/mperks), and you'll receive a $2 coupon off your next Meijer shopping trip just for signing up. You must agree to receive text messages from Meijer in order to receive the service.

mPerks, though, doesn't really know what it wants to be. While you need to provide your cell number, and will get coupon alerts via text, you actually need to clip the coupons from the mPerks website—which you can do from your home computer. While you log in to mPerks to clip digital coupons, you enter your cellphone number at checkout to receive these discounts.

Meijer is also known for sending out random mPerks rewards to users (such as $2 or $5 off your next shopping trip), so it's worth logging in regularly to see what's available.

Meijer now includes both store and manufacturer coupons on mPerks. You can stack store mPerks coupons at Meijer with paper manufacturer coupons, just as you can the printable Meijer MealBox store coupons, so always be on the lookout for ways to stack your savings. Manufacturer mPerks coupons, however, cannot be stacked. Roll your mouse over each coupon on Meijer's website and the popup will tell you whether it is a store or manufacturer mobile coupon.

Hy-Vee Mobile Alerts

Sign up for SMS alerts from Hy-Vee, including hot deals and special promotions (www.hy-vee.com/company/mobile-alerts.aspx). You also can opt into NOWWOW coupons via text, which are time-sensitive alerts of mobile coupons good for limited hours on a specific day.

Redbox Text Club

Redbox kiosks are found at many grocery stores, Walgreens, and McDonald's, and offer one-night DVD rentals for $1. Sign up to receive texts from Redbox (www.redbox.com/textclub) and they'll send you a free one-night DVD rental code during the first week of each month, plus additional random codes and offers.

> **TIPS AND TRICKS**
>
> Beyond the free rental codes, services like Redbox offer great entertainment alternatives. Many people are able to drop cable with little pain, when they combine over-the-air TV with rental kiosk services like Redbox or Blockbuster Express, DVD loans from their local library, and a streaming service such as Netflix (www.Netflix.com).

Also sign up for Redbox e-mails at Redbox.com. They'll send you info on new releases, plus occasional special offers, including free DVD rental codes for your anniversary with them and more.

ShopText

If you're interested in receiving various coupons and freebies via postal mail, sign up with ShopText (consumer.shoptext.com). Various companies run coupon or free sample promos through ShopText. Simply text the designated code word to the shortcode 467467 in order to receive that freebie or coupon offer via postal mail. Sign up for ShopText online, and they'll text some of these offers to you.

You'll also sometimes see ShopText offers listed in magazines (most often fashion and women's magazines). Keep an eye out for ShopText offers in ads and articles.

ShopText keeps your info on file, so when you text for coupons they automatically send to the address linked to your cell number.

Target Mobile Coupons

Sign up for Target mobile coupons (sites.target.com/site/en/spot/page.jsp?title=text_alerts), and you'll receive a weekly text message alerting you to new coupons. Click on the link in the text, and these coupons display as a web page through the browser on your smartphone.

Your cashier can scan the barcode right off of your phone at the store, which automatically deducts the mobile coupon for each of the products you're purchasing. These are always store coupons, so can be stacked with paper manufacturer coupons for a better deal.

Even though Target mobile coupons actually display through your mobile web browser, not SMS, there is no way to access them without agreeing to receive text messages from Target. If you want to print them out from a home computer, you'll have to type in the very long web address from your phone.

Keep an eye on the register when they scan your phone, because sometimes these mobile coupons have been known not to come off properly. Sometimes they are also valid only on select sizes and varieties, which aren't spelled out well on the small screen.

Mobile Apps from Stores

You'll also want to look for mobile apps for your favorite stores, as these often offer coupons or discounts just for downloading or using the app. If you're a frequent Barnes & Noble shopper, for instance, be sure to grab their app; if you are often found in Target, download theirs. Think of your favorite stores and do a search in your device's app store or mobile marketplace to see if they have an associated app.

Mobile Coupon and Shopping Apps

In addition to e-coupon apps that match up with the electronic coupon websites, there are a number of other mobile shopping and coupon apps, both for grocery purchases and other retail chains. Some fancier apps are paid, but you can do an awful lot with mobile apps for free. Following, find a number of free apps you might want to check out.

CardStar

Tired of keeping track of all your loyalty cards and key tags? CardStar (mycardstar.com) lets users load all of their loyalty, rewards, and club cards onto their smartphone. Just enter your membership number off each card, and CardStar creates a scannable barcode image right on your phone.

TIPS AND TRICKS

Don't have a smartphone? CardStar also lets you consolidate up to six membership and rewards cards onto a single printed card, reducing the number of cards you need to bring with you to the store. While the app is free, there is a charge for this physical card. (Currently $5.95 for one card, with discounts for additional cards.) Visit mycardstar.com/cardstarcard. html to get started.

CardStar also provides deals, coupons, and exclusive offers for your local stores.

CheckPoints

Earn rewards for window shopping! Check in with CheckPoints (www.checkpoints.com) at local stores, and earn points that you can redeem for prizes like Amazon gift cards, airline miles, and electronics. You can also earn bonus coins by scanning products, then use the coins to play games where you can win more points. (This is a good way to keep older kids busy in the store—give them your phone and send them off to scan all the designated products and earn coins while you're shopping.)

Coupon Sherpa

Available only for iPhone or iPod Touch, Coupon Sherpa (www. couponsherpa.com/mobile-coupons) offers location-based retail coupons for both stores and restaurants, as well as exclusive codes for mobile users. Open up the app while you're out and about, and it will tell you what coupons are available for nearby stores.

Facebook Places

Facebook Places (www.facebook.com/places) is a geolocation app that allows users to check in at various places. Check-ins appear in the app, on your Facebook Wall, and the newsfeed of your Facebook friends, and you can also tag other Facebook friends who are at the same location and see who else is nearby at the same time.

While Facebook Places is only partially a deals app, companies have caught on to the power of geolocation. Users will see a "deal" logo on their phone when checking in at a location where a deal is available. There are several types of Facebook Places deals, including:

- Individual—Deals offered by local businesses to users who check in with Facebook Places.

- Friend—Tag a given number of friends at a certain location, and you all share the savings.

- Loyalty—Check in multiple times at the same location, and they may reward you with a repeat-customer discount.

Facebook Places competes mainly with Foursquare, explained next.

Foursquare

Foursquare (foursquare.com) is another geolocation app where users can check in to places and share their locations with their friends. Some local businesses and restaurants offer discounts or freebies to anyone who shows that they have checked in with Foursquare, such as a free appetizer.

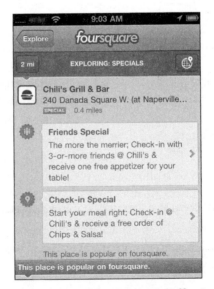

Foursquare sometimes gives special offers just for checking in at a given location.

Other businesses offer random discounts or offers to attract Foursquare users. Whole Foods, for instance, has offered such perks as a free half-gallon of Organic Valley milk to people who have checked in with Foursquare. Great Clips has run sweepstakes that are only open to users who have checked in with Foursquare.

GeoQpons

GeoQpons (www.geoqpons.com) is a location-based coupon service that gives you mobile coupons for retail stores, largely at the mall— you can let the cashier scan the barcode or enter the code off of your phone, or e-mail the coupons to yourself to print out and bring to the store. Browse coupons available at your local stores or look under Brands/Retail coupons to see those available for specific brands, both in-store and online.

Grocery iQ

Grocery iQ (www.groceryiq.com) lets you create grocery shopping lists, print coupons for your items from your list, organize by aisle, and more. You can also scan barcodes in the store with your phone to create a list for later.

RedLaser

RedLaser (redlaser.com) is a barcode scanning application with multiple uses:

- Compare prices (using TheFind, Google Product Search, eBay, and Half.com).

- Find the product you're looking for in nearby stores.

- Check for allergen information and nutrition facts.

- Scan a book's barcode at a bookstore to see if a local library carries it.

- Send barcodes to yourself by e-mail while shopping to create a list of items to check out later.

RedLaser only works on newer phones.

Shopkick

Shopkick (shopkick.com) offers coupons and deals at thousands of brick-and-mortar stores—but also rewards you just for visiting! Open the Shopkick app when you walk into a participating store, and you'll earn rewards, or "kicks."

Earn "kicks" by using Shopkick at various stores, then redeem for rewards.

Scan the barcodes of participating featured products at participating stores, and you'll earn rewards. Cash in those rewards for anything from gift cards to movie tickets.

ShopSavvy

You can also find comparison-shopping mobile apps to help you find the best price on items when you're out and about. Let's say you're standing in Best Buy and they have a sale running on a new Disney DVD your kids really want to see. But you're not sure if Target or Walmart or Amazon might have a better price, or if you really want to buy it today. Use an app like ShopSavvy (shopsavvy.mobi) to scan the product's barcode. ShopSavvy will give you its current price, both at local stores and online, and will also show user reviews of that item.

Yowza!!

Yowza!! (www.getyowza.com) provides location-based mobile coupons for retail stores and restaurants. It uses the geolocation features of your phone to show you available coupons for stores near you, and you can simply show your cashier the e-coupon on your phone so she can scan the barcode or punch in a code to give you your discount.

Coupons via QR Codes

Quick Response (QR) codes are special barcodes that can store information such as web addresses. When a mobile phone user scans the QR code with a QR-scanner app, the information contained in that code is automatically delivered to their phone.

Businesses are placing QR codes around their stores or in magazines or other media more and more often. Visitors can simply scan the QR code with their phone to receive a coupon, additional information, or an invitation to check in with a service like Foursquare—without having to type in a web address or text the company for information.

Scan QR codes to bring up coupons or info on your smartphone.

TIPS AND TRICKS

While there are a number of QR apps, two popular fast and free options are NeoReader (neoreader.com) and RedLaser (redlaser.com; see more info earlier in this chapter). Both can read not only QR codes, but UPC and other barcode types. Note that some readers don't work as well on older phones or older operating systems.

QR scanners use a phone's built-in camera to take a photo of the code, and then read the information it contains. You'll need a smartphone with a camera to use these.

Privacy Concerns

Mobile apps and texts, along with electronic coupons and online personalized deals, allow stores and manufacturers to track consumers' purchasing and couponing patterns. In the case of geolocation apps, they can also keep track of the dates and times of all your visits to various stores!

Companies and stores try to present this as a plus for consumers, allowing them to offer you more targeted coupons and other offers.

For instance, if you often purchase Brand A cat food, you might receive a mobile or e-coupon offer for Brand A cat food—or, you might instead receive one for Brand B cat food in an effort to entice you to switch. This is similar to the coupons that print out at the register for another brand right after you purchase a competing product.

This tracking of your purchasing patterns, however, does raise privacy concerns. How much do you want companies to know about you, and how aware are you of where this information is going and how it is being used? Cynical-minded couponers also worry that this type of tracking allows manufacturers to offer fewer discounts on items, because they can see over time that you're likely to purchase these anyway, coupon or no coupon.

The use of tracking information for creating personalized electronic coupons also strikes at the heart of couponers' ability to share information with each other.

If I find a great deal at the store, but it depends on an electronic coupon or personalized price that's tied to my loyalty card or my personalized instance of a mobile app, then I can't tell you about that deal—there's really no point, if you don't have the same personalized offer.

Information sharing is the great strength of couponing in the information age, so this development is worrisome for couponers and worth keeping an eye on.

The Least You Need to Know

- Stores and manufacturers are experimenting with mobile coupons and apps to reach consumers in new ways.
- Grab freebies and coupons via text, but make sure you have a monthly or unlimited text plan on your phone.
- Be aware of what information you're giving out about your shopping habits and how this might be used.

Online Coupon Codes and Bonus Discounts

In This Chapter

- Maximize Amazon savings
- Get discount gift cards to stretch your dollars further
- Use coupon codes for extra savings
- Extra sneaky discounts through savvy strategies
- Comparison shop around for the best deals

If couponing is a sport, we need to have a lot of moves at our disposal, and they all work together to keep us at the top of our game. From comparison shopping online to ensure you get the best deal (at Amazon or anywhere else!) to stacking up your savings, maximize your online savings by shopping strategically.

Amazon is big because it offers users great deals and a good shopping experience, but the biggies should be just part of your online shopping strategy. Here, find out about saving on all your online purchases through coupon codes—and beyond.

Amazon

The proverbial 800-pound gorilla in the room, Amazon has moved well beyond books to offer deals on everything from electronics to toys to groceries and drugstore staples that often rival (or even beat) those at local stores. Amazon also offers fantastic deals on specialty items, and can be a lifesaver for shoppers in rural areas where stores face less competition and less pressure to keep prices down.

Amazon Coupons and Codes

You won't find Amazon coupon codes on large coupon code sites like RetailMeNot (see discussion later in this chapter). However, you will find Amazon coupons and codes on Amazon itself. They keep these pretty well hidden, so here's how to get to them.

First, be sure you are logged in to your Amazon account so that you can see and clip coupons. Sometimes you'll see a coupon right on the middle of a specific item page. But to see a whole list of coupons to clip into your account, click "Today's Deals" at the top of the Amazon home page, then click "Coupons" at the top of the next page. Then just click any coupon you want to clip into your account.

Once you have clipped a coupon, it remains in your account and automatically comes off at checkout when you buy a qualifying product. You won't see the coupon discount come off until the final page of checkout, right before you place your order.

TIPS AND TRICKS

Be sure to scroll through the entire list of coupons under each category. Sometimes several pages are available, and you can't see all the coupons on the first screen.

Most coupons on Amazon reset monthly, and can be clipped and used only once per account.

Beyond coupons you can clip into your account, Amazon also offers coupon codes that you can enter on the last checkout screen— most often on food and beverage items. To find these codes, go to the Amazon home page, click "Shop All Departments," then click "Grocery & Gourmet Food."

Click "Special Offers" on the top right of the screen and you'll see a whole list of specials on various products. Click any product to see the monthly discount code. You can often combine these codes with Subscribe & Save discounts, which are explained in the next section.

Subscribe & Save

Subscribe & Save works pretty much the way it sounds. When you subscribe to have an eligible item from Amazon shipped to you automatically at regular intervals, you get an automatic 15 percent off your purchase, plus free shipping.

HEADS-UP

Be sure to cancel Subscribe & Save at some point if you don't want items to keep coming—at whatever price Amazon is currently charging. Subscribe & Save locks in an item for delivery; it does not lock in a price. You can cancel at any time with no penalty, just choose the manage subscriptions options under your Amazon account and cancel each. A good time to do this is when the first shipment arrives; use this as your reminder to cancel.

If an item is eligible for Subscribe & Save, you'll see a notice in a blue box in the middle of the item description page. Over on the right, you have the option of one-time delivery (simply purchasing the item) or subscribing to receive the item at regular intervals.

Choosing the subscription option activates your subscription, and you'll see the 15 percent Subscribe & Save discount plus your free shipping discount come off on the final page of checkout.

Whenever you see the Subscribe & Save option: take it! For 15 percent off and free shipping, why not? Also be on the lookout for codes and coupons for Subscribe & Save items, since you can stack these for additional discounts.

Amazon Mom and Amazon Student

Amazon Mom (www.amazon.com/gp/mom/signup/info) and Amazon Student (www.amazon.com/gp/student/signup/info) offer special discounts for caregivers and registered students, respectively. Both are free programs.

Amazon Mom members (who don't need to be moms; the program is for all caregivers) get an automatic 15 percent off select diapers and wipes, plus an additional 5 percent off with Subscribe & Save.

These stack off the original price, giving 20 percent off in total. New Amazon Mom sign-ups receive three free months of Amazon Prime (free two-day shipping on qualifying items) as well as three months of these special discounts. In order to maintain your Amazon Mom discounts after the three-month introductory period, you'll need to sign up for Amazon Prime at a cost of $79 per year. If you haven't yet joined the Amazon Mom program, you can think about signing up and stocking up heavily on diapers during that free three-month period.

Amazon Student members must currently be enrolled in a college or university and have a valid .edu e-mail address. They receive a free year of Amazon Prime, plus additional occasional discounts and promotions on items like textbooks, dorm room supplies, and sometimes even video games or MP3s.

Gold Box and Lightning Deals

Each day, Amazon offers one heavily discounted "Gold Box" deal all day or until it sells out. Lightning deals each run for a couple of hours or until they sell out, and change over all day. Click "Today's Deals" at the top of the Amazon home page to view Gold Box and Lightning deals.

Friday Sale

Each week, Amazon offers several pages of special discounts at their one-day-only Friday sales (www.amazon.com/Friday-Sale/b?ie=UTF8&node=548166). If items sell out before the end of the day, they're gone, so make a point of browsing early.

TIPS AND TRICKS

Amazon's Friday sale is a great place to find discounts on coffee (including K-Cups for Keurig brewers) and organic food and beverage items.

Friday sales start at 12 A.M. Pacific time, if you're up and want to get a head start.

Amazon Warehouse Deals

At Amazon Warehouse Deals (www.amazon.com/
b?ie=UTF8&node=1267877011), find deep discounts on returned,
open box, or near-expiration products. Usually these items are
offered in very limited quantities, so browse through their categories
and see what strikes your fancy.

Discount Gift Cards

You can find discounted gift cards online for Amazon as well as
for other virtual or brick-and-mortar retailers. If you're planning a
major purchase at a specific store, you can grab yourself a gift card at
a discount and use that to pay.

Online

Several sites allow users to buy and sell unwanted gift cards at a
discount. If Aunt Mildred buys you a gift card for Christmas to a
store you'd never set foot in, you can sell it to one of these sites for
cash, or for Amazon credit.

If you're looking to make a major purchase, or if you shop at certain stores all the time, you can check these sites for discounted gift
cards. Use those gift cards to pay for your item, and you've given
yourself an automatic discount off your purchase, usually ranging
from 7 to 15 percent.

Sites to check out include:

- Cardpool—www.cardpool.com
- Craigslist—craigslist.org; do a search for "gift card" in the
  for sale/wanted section of your local Craigslist.
- GiftCardBin—giftcardbin.com
- GiftCardRescue—www.giftcardrescue.com
- Plastic Jungle—www.plasticjungle.com

Each site guarantees that these "used" gift cards contain the dollar amount advertised. Since their inventory depends on cards others have sold to these sites, you can check several to see who has a card for the store you're looking for. Sites like Gift Card Granny (www. giftcardgranny.com) aggregate available cards across multiple sites, but aren't always up to date, so it's better to visit the sites yourself.

> **TIPS AND TRICKS**
>
> People also resell gift cards on eBay, so check there, too. Oddly though, buyers tend to bid these up close to the gift card's value, so you may find a better discount at the gift card reseller sites. Also watch out for people selling used "no value" limited-edition gift cards as collectibles.

Since these sites depend on people selling unused gift cards, their inventory constantly changes. If you don't see the card you need, check back or sign up for e-mail alerts when a retailer or restaurant of interest becomes available.

Catalinas

Grocery stores sometimes run on-your-next-order Catalina offers on gift card purchases. You'll see these especially around traditional gift-giving holidays like Mother's Day, Father's Day, and Christmas—but you don't have to get them as gifts. Buy some for yourself! When you purchase gift cards to stores you'll be shopping at anyway, you've just gotten a bonus of free groceries.

Local grocery stores may, for instance, offer back a $10 Catalina on a $50 gift card purchase, or a $20 Catalina on a $100 gift card purchase. Read the fine print, because sometimes you can purchase any card from the gift card mall, or kiosk of gift cards for various retailers, while other times it's limited to select retailers.

Coupon and Free Shipping Codes

You'll want to search for coupon codes that give a percent off your purchases or free shipping—whenever and wherever you shop online.

If you're planning on making the purchase anyway, you'll want to get it as cheaply as possible.

HEADS-UP

Sometimes coupon-code discounts don't show up until the last page of checkout, so don't panic—but also don't hit submit until you're sure that the discount has come off your total.

Many of these codes are shared by customers, so if you get a non-unique code by mail or e-mail, you can also share it with others. Some online retailers restrict "customer submitted codes" and have told the coupon-code sites to cease and desist from sharing discount codes. You'll see a message to that effect when you search.

When you're ready to check out from an online retailer, just keep the page with your shopping cart open in a tab in your web browser. Hit Ctrl-T (Command-T on a Mac) to open a separate tab for coupon-code sites. As you search these sites, you can easily click back over to the open tab with your shopping cart to try out the codes. (Don't retype them—just highlight and copy using Ctrl-C on a PC or Command-C on a Mac, then click in the code box on the retailer site and hit Ctrl-V on a PC or Command-V on a Mac to copy.)

It won't take more than a couple of minutes to click through and search—couponing doesn't have to be time consuming or difficult. Visitors to coupon-code sites generally don't spend more than a minute or two searching, and save an average of around $20 an order. $20 for two minutes of your time is worth the bother.

As with the cash-back sites, it's often useful to check more than one coupon-code site, since one might list a code others don't, or might have a higher-value code.

RetailMeNot

RetailMeNot (www.retailmenot.com) is one of the best and most well-known sites for finding coupon and free shipping codes. Users can report back on whether codes worked, and each code displays both a percentage of success and when the code was first submitted so that you can try the more recent and successful codes first.

Their home page always shows the day's top coupons, and you can sign up for regular e-mail newsletters of popular codes. Be careful that these don't lead to impulse buys—use codes on items you were already planning to purchase, rather than going on a shopping spree because the code creates a sale.

Beyond online codes, RetailMeNot also contains some printable coupons for brick-and-mortar stores. So for instance, if you look up JC Penney on RetailMeNot, you'll find both coupon codes for use when shopping online and printable coupons for use when shopping in store. JC Penney almost always has a printable 15 percent off or $10/$50 coupon online, and many other retailers post similar offers. Print some coupons out before your next mall trip to save on your shopping.

> **TIPS AND TRICKS**
>
> Also use sites like RetailMeNot to find restaurant discount codes for carry-out or delivery. Restaurants that offer online ordering often release these codes, so search for anything from Domino's Pizza to Smokey Bones and use coupon codes to save. RetailMeNot also contains printable coupons for many restaurants, just as it does for brick-and-mortar retailers.

Have a new code or printable coupon to share? Submit it through the handy form in RetailMeNot's right-hand sidebar. Give back to the coupon community by sharing your finds with others.

Coupon Cabin

If you don't find the code you're looking for on RetailMeNot, try Coupon Cabin (www.couponcabin.com), where you can also sign up to receive daily e-mails of their top coupon codes. Coupon Cabin is another great place to browse, since they display each day's top coupons right on the home page. Gold stars indicate coupons guaranteed to work.

Coupon Cabin also offers exclusive weekly high-value Coupon Club offers. Rather than displaying the code on their site, they make you sign up via e-mail. When enough people sign up, everyone receives the code via e-mail.

Lastly, if you do a lot of online shopping you can easily add the Coupon Cabin bookmarklet, or little bookmark code, to your Favorites or Bookmarks in your web browser. When you're on the site of any online retailer, you simply click the bookmarklet and it will automatically pop open a window containing any available codes for the site you're visiting.

Cash-Back Sites

Most of the cash-back sites we talked about in Chapter 9 also offer coupon codes for participating retailers. This is a great way to stack a code with a cash-back offer, since codes found directly on the cash-back sites are guaranteed to work with the cash back, while codes found on external sites may not.

Many sites will also automatically "clip" the code when you click through, so you don't have to copy it manually when you check out.

FreeShipping.org

FreeShipping.org works pretty much the way it sounds: search for an online retailer, and they'll tell you if there's a free shipping code available. Some of the offers have restrictions, such as free shipping with a purchase of $50 or more, or free shipping on shoes, so read through to see what applies to your purchase.

Retailer Sites

Retailers often post discount codes right on their home pages, but sometimes these are easy to miss when you're fixated on finding a specific product or distracted by their advertising. Poke around the home page to see if they're advertising a specific deal.

Also be sure to sign up for e-mail newsletters at each of your favorite online retailers. Many e-mail regular discount codes to subscribers, or e-mail a welcome promotion to new e-mail sign-ups.

Combining Codes

Some sites let you stack two or more codes, so you can get both free shipping and a percent-off discount. So don't stop with just one code—try to use both codes! Other sites only allow one code per transaction, so you'll want to use whichever gives the biggest discount.

> **COUPON QUIPS**
>
> Coupon codes can sometimes get you cheap groceries at sites you'd never expect. If you have a Kohl's card, for example, you can often find 30 percent off and free shipping codes for sites like Kohls.com. Kohl's carries K-Cups, and lets you stack two codes. Stacking a sale with a 30 percent code and a free shipping code can sometimes get you K-Cups shipped from Kohl's more cheaply than at local grocery stores.

Even if there's only one coupon code box, enter one, apply it, then enter a second and apply. If it replaces the first code, you'll know you can only use one.

Stack Your Savings

Just as you stack your savings at grocery stores and drugstores, you want to stack savings on all your online purchases as well. When buying a discount gift card online, for instance, think about multiple ways to save on a single item. This can especially add up when you're making a major purchase. Let's say you want to buy a new $600 washing machine from Home Depot (plus 6.5 percent sales tax and a $69 delivery charge).

If you simply walked into your local store and charged this purchase, you would pay $708 after taxes and delivery fee. But let's see what happens when you stack up the savings online instead:

- Pay $558 at Plastic Jungle for a $600 Home Depot gift card at 7 percent off face value, saving $42.

- Use a cash-back credit card to get 1 percent cash back on your gift card purchase, for $5.58 in your cash-back rewards account.

- Use RetailMeNot to find a 15 percent off code for Home Depot, dropping the price to $510, saving $90.

- Save $5.85 in tax after coupon code (6.5 percent tax on $510 is $33.15; 6.5 percent tax on $600 is $39).

- Go through eBates for 3 percent cash back on your $510 washing machine purchase, earning $15.30.

- Find a delivery charge rebate form on the Home Depot website, and get back that $69 delivery fee.

Let's add it up!

$510.00 washing machine after code
+$33.15 sales tax
+$69.00 delivery fee

$612.15

Pay that $612.15 with the $600 gift card from Plastic Jungle + $12.15 on Discover (earning another whopping $.12 cash back). But you only paid $558 for the gift card, so your actual out-of-pocket cost here is $570.15.

But let's not forget our cash back!

 $5.70 cash back from Discover
+$15.30 cash back from Ebates
+$69.00 delivery charge rebate back from Home Depot

 $90.00

So you've paid $570.15 out of pocket, but you will be receiving $90 back in cash-back bonus and rebates. This makes your net cost for this washing machine $480.15.

HEADS-UP

When using a cash-back site, always start there for coupon codes. Sometimes when you use an outside code from a site like RetailMeNot, it invalidates the cash back. When you use a code from the cash-back site, you are guaranteed to get the cash back. Codes almost always give you better savings than cash-back sites, though, so if your code is 15 percent and your cash back is only 5 percent, use the code and take your chances.

You've just saved $227.85 on a major purchase, when compared to the $708 you would have paid in-store. That's worth the bit of extra time it takes to go through these steps!

Sneak Yourself a Discount

Let's say you're unable to find a discount code to use on an online item, but you really want to buy it. Here are a couple of ideas to try.

Join Up

First, sign up for an online retailer's e-mails before you buy. If this is a site you haven't shopped before, they may send you an introductory offer via e-mail. Many sites offer 10 percent or 15 percent discount codes to new sign-ups. Leave your cart open in one window, sign up for e-mails in another, and wait a bit to see what you receive.

Lay in Wait

Create an account on a retailer's site, then put an item in your cart and leave it there. They may notice that you've gone through the process and bailed at the last minute. Some sites may e-mail a code, or a representative may pop up a chat window and offer you an incentive to complete the purchase.

COUPON QUIPS

Waiting works especially well on photo sites. More than once I've created a photo book, balked at the price at checkout, left it in my cart to think about it, and a couple of days later received a percent-off code via e-mail.

This of course works best on sites where items are less likely to sell out. But if you don't find a discount code today, and you aren't in a hurry, wait a bit—you never know when a new discount code might appear either by e-mail or on a site like RetailMeNot tomorrow.

Chat Them Up

Many sites now offer prominent links to live online chats with sales representatives. If you have items in your cart but can't find a code, open up a chat window and ask if there are any available codes for your purchases today. It never hurts to ask! This has worked for me on sites like Lands' End, where the last time I tried it the representative offered me a free shipping code.

Try eBay

People do sell their coupon codes and offers on eBay. Let's say, for instance, you're planning on making a $60 purchase at Gymboree. com. Do a search for Gymbucks on eBay, and you'll find people selling their $25 off a $50 purchase Gymbucks (good online and in store) for under $7. If you spend $7 to save $25, you're still up $18.

Check eBay for everything from Amazon codes (usually from advertising-supported Kindles) to codes for office supply stores—but make sure first that the code sellers are offering isn't already out there for free "in the wild" on sites like RetailMeNot. Check the eBay seller's feedback rating to be sure they're trustworthy before you buy.

Comparison Shopping

You'll want to be sure you're getting the best deal on anything you buy, both online and offline. Comparison shopping sites let you search for a specific product and see a list of what your final shipped price will be at a number of sites.

These sites work best when you have a specific model number or very specific item to compare—"Disney Epic Mickey," for example, as opposed to "red shirt."

> **TIPS AND TRICKS**
>
> Comparison shopping sites don't account for discount codes or cash back, so your true final price might be less when you take those into consideration.

Comparison sites work basically the same way: enter a product into their search box; see a list of prices at various online retailers. Start your search at sites like Nextag (www.nextag.com) and PriceGrabber (www.pricegrabber.com).

The Least You Need to Know

- Many offers on Amazon can help you save.
- Stack up your savings from discount gift cards, coupon codes, and more; sneak a discount when none seems available.
- Comparison shop to ensure you're getting the best deal.

Planning and Organizing

Couponing can seem overwhelming, but it doesn't have to be. A little planning, a little organizing, and you'll get into the rhythm of integrating couponing into your daily life with minimum effort. Part 4 starts with an outline of how to acquire more coupons for the items you love—and how to organize those coupons for effective trips to the store.

Then we jump back online and embrace the power of the internet-couponing community; from blogs to forums to Facebook, the info you need is right at your fingers. Why reinvent the wheel, when you can learn about the deals and coupon matchups from others who are out there doing a lot of the work for you. We'll then put it all together and talk about how to combine your online knowledge with all the strategies you've picked up to plan out the best shopping trips of your life.

Effective couponing depends on you buying the right items for your family's needs, so we'll move on to ways to coupon for your priorities. Whether you prefer to eat organic or live in a rural area with less competition or options, there are strategies to help you save. And when you bring it home, find out the best ways to organize your items and where to donate your bounty to help others.

We'll wrap up with a look at the future of couponing, and what changing policies mean to us as couponers.

Acquiring and Organizing Coupons

In This Chapter

- Where to get more coupons to maximize your savings
- Companies that reward you for spreading the word about their products
- Corralling your coupons

Now that you've seen some of the ways you can save, both on- and offline, how do you go about acquiring and organizing the paper coupons that will help you build your stockpile? When you start playing the couponing game by stocking up on multiple items as they hit their lowest price point, you will start to need multiple coupons for these items. But when you start acquiring multiple coupons, it's easy to get overwhelmed by all the paper.

In this chapter, find out where to get more coupons and how to organize them for easy planning before you go to the store.

Finding More Coupons

As we've talked about from the beginning, sometimes you need to buy in larger quantities to save the most. To save even more on these types of sales, you want to use a coupon on every item you buy, which sometimes means that you need multiples of the same coupons. You also need a good variety of coupons in your stash, so that you're prepared to match them up with the different store sales that come along. Here are some strategies for bulking up your coupon collection.

Get Multiple Papers

If you live in a large urban or suburban area where your local newspaper contains a good number of coupons, consider buying multiple Sunday-only subscriptions to the largest-circulation paper in your area. Most newspapers allow more than one subscription per household, although you may have to put each in a different name—this is more sales for them!

It's often cheaper per paper to subscribe than to pick these up at the store. Think here about what your investment is worth. If you spend $.75 a week per subscription, and get two subscriptions, you only have to use $1.50 a week in coupons to make back that investment. Everything after that is pure profit.

> **COUPON QUIPS**
>
> Look online for coupon codes to get your Sunday newspaper subscriptions at a discount; these are often available on local coupon blogs or on sites like RetailMeNot.com. Discount subscriptions also sometimes pop up on daily deals sites like Groupon, which has, for example, offered the Sunday *Chicago Tribune* for $.25 a week (as opposed to its normal $1.00 a week).

If your noncouponing neighbors and friends subscribe, also see if they're willing to save their coupon inserts for you. You can offer to pick up a few of their favorite items for free or for cheap with coupons on occasion to help pay them back.

On a good coupon week, you might want to pick up additional newspapers at the store. See what stores in your area sell the Sunday paper at a discount: Dollar Tree, Deals, and Menards often do.

eBay

eBay is a great source for extra coupons, plus a place to pick up coupons that were only distributed regionally or a higher value than you receive in your local coupon inserts. To find coupons on eBay, just do a search for the product's name plus the word coupons: "Crest coupons" or "Purex coupons," for example.

You can also find entire Sunday coupon inserts on eBay. This is especially useful if you live in a rural area and your local newspaper lacks inserts or has few coupons. Just search for the date plus the word *inserts*: "7/24 inserts," for example. Most sellers list the coupons and values in the insert so you can see if they're worth to you what the seller is asking.

Sellers on eBay and elsewhere note that you're paying for their time to clip the coupons or their time to find, package, and ship the inserts, rather than for the coupons themselves. Why? Look in the fine print on most manufacturer coupons, and they'll say void if transferred or sold.

So far, this has worked for both sellers and buyers—the coupon is the same coupon whether you get it on eBay, clip it from the paper, or find it on the floor. Your local store will be reimbursed no matter where you got it.

Look at your seller's rating before you buy; you want the seller to have a lot of sales, and a lot of positive feedback. If you're looking for quick coupons for a current sale, you can also switch to looking at only "buy it now" auctions. Most item descriptions say when the person will ship and where the coupons will ship from, so you can estimate whether you'll receive them on time.

Coupon Clippers

Because so many people use eBay, coupon prices can be somewhat higher there (and be sure to factor in shipping!). Coupon clipping services, or clippers, specialize in clipped coupons and/or entire inserts. They sometimes offer better deals or have more consistent stock. Most also offer rewards programs, where you earn points or credits for purchases that you can redeem on later purchases.

When you visit a coupon clipping service's website, you can search for coupons for specific products or inserts from specific dates.

Clippers offer each for a price, plus a per-order shipping and handling fee. As with eBay, make sure your anticipated savings from the coupons you acquire on clipper sites are higher than your cost to pick up the coupons.

To maximize those rewards, pick one or two clippers to use. Also look for someone reasonably close to you, since you'll receive coupons faster if they don't have to travel as far. There are hundreds of clippers to choose from, but here are a few to get you started:

- Coupon Dede's—coupondede.com
- The Coupon Clippers—thecouponclippers.com
- Insert Insanity—insertinsanity.com

Some services offer entire uncut inserts, in addition to clipped coupons. This is useful if you missed buying a paper one week, or live in an area where Sunday inserts are sparse or nonexistent.

Coupon Swaps

Another strategy is to swap coupons with others, both on- and offline. This simply makes sense—I have a cat, you have a baby, so why don't I trade you my diaper coupons for your pet food coupons?

Many large coupon forums (which we'll discuss in Chapter 15) have subforums devoted to coupon trading. Community members list the coupons they're looking for and the coupons they have to trade, and you can contact them privately and go from there. These sites also have a rating program similar to eBay's, where you can rate the traders. Try to swap with users who have high feedback ratings.

Also look into local coupon swaps. Some public libraries host these regularly. If yours does not, ask them about starting one or using their meeting room to start your own. Some libraries have boxes out where people can leave unwanted coupons and exchange for coupons others have left. You might get together with friends once a month and swap coupons you've collected, or collect gluten-free coupons for a friend who collects cereal coupons for you.

Coupon Trains

You can also exchange coupons with others by joining or starting a *coupon train*. Here, the first person on the "train" mails an envelope full of clipped coupons to the next member, who pulls out the ones she wants, tosses any that are expired, and replaces with an equal number of coupons. She then mails the coupons to the next person on the train, who repeats the process.

TIPS AND TRICKS

Be a courteous participant. If you pull out high-value coupons, don't re-place them with junky ones that the other riders on your train are unlikely to want. Send the envelope on immediately rather than holding on to it.

Find a train to join on one of the coupon forums listed in Chapter 15, or start your own with friends across the country. Trains work best with about 7 to 8 participants—enough to make it worth everyone's while, but not so many that it takes too much time to wind around to the beginning again. It's also best to have riders in different states so that you can share regional coupons.

Contact Companies

We generally don't think to contact companies unless we have a complaint. Because they get so many complaints, though, manufacturers are often very responsive to compliments.

Visit the website of any brand or manufacturer and look for a "contact us" link. Drop them a note telling them how much you or your children or your dog enjoy their products, add a question about whether they'll have new coupons available any time soon, and include your address.

Not every company will send out coupons for compliments, but many do. It's cheaper for them to keep you as a loyal customer than to go out and find new customers, so they often will offer a couple of coupons to keep you happy. Since it takes but a minute or two to jot down one of these e-mails or fill out a form, try contacting a company or two a day. Within a few weeks, you should be receiving coupons in your mailbox.

You can also do this if you have a complaint about a product. I had a tube of Pillsbury dough, for instance, pop open in my refrigerator. I complained; they sent me coupons for free products. A friend bought a defective pack of Huggies diapers and the tabs tore off when she tried to use them. She complained; they sent her several coupons for free replacement packages.

COUPON QUIPS

Companies usually reset their databases every three months or so. If you've written successfully for coupons in the past, wait a few months and try again.

Not sure what to write or who to contact? Check out sample letters and ideas for companies to contact at Couponing to Disney's "five-a-day" campaign here: www.couponingtodisney.com/category/5-a-day.

Word-of-Mouth Marketing Sites

Companies know we tune out ads and marketing messages, preferring to get info from our friends. So when you sign up for these types of sites, they'll occasionally send out high-value coupons for new products, samples, or coupons for free products, plus additional coupons for you to share with your friends.

Some of these sites are run by companies themselves, such as Kraft First Taste. Others, such as SheSpeaks, work with a variety of different manufacturers. Sign up for as many as possible, as each offers a different mix of coupons and free samples. Here are a few to get you started:

- BzzAgent—www.bzzagent.com
- Kraft First Taste—www.kraftfirsttaste.com

- SheSpeaks—www.shespeaks.com
- Smiley306—smiley360.com
- Tryology—www.expotv.com/tryology
- Viewpoints—www.viewpoints.com
- Vocalpoint—www.vocalpoint.com

Some sites just send out random coupons; others send out e-mail invitations and you need to sign up to participate. After you receive your coupon or sample and have had a chance to try the product, these sites generally ask you to come back to do a review.

> **COUPON QUIPS**
>
> Beyond coupons and samples, these marketing sites often contain entire online communities, discussions, surveys, and more. The more active you are on a site and in their various product campaigns, the more likely you are to be invited to participate in future campaigns. Since they want to spread the word about new products, they value activity and discussion.

Sign up for every one of these sites. Even if they only mail you coupons every couple of months or so, they tend to send coupons for free products or high-value coupons, and sometimes full-size samples. (Again, use your alternate e-mail account for these.)

Organizing Your Coupons

You can see that as you start exploring these various methods you might end up with an awful lot of coupons to corral. So how do you keep them organized so you can find them quickly while planning out your shopping trips?

The Clip-Free Method

When you start looking at acquiring multiple Sunday newspapers and organizing all of the coupons that have suddenly come into your life, the process can seem a bit overwhelming. Especially if you're new to couponing, start with the clip-free method and simplify your life.

Each week when you get your newspaper inserts, write the date on the front really big. (Unless you enjoy deciphering the microscopic date printed on the spine!) Then, file these in an accordion folder or in hanging file folders, arranged by date. Have the newest inserts always at the front.

TIPS AND TRICKS

Use a site like CouponTom.com (coupontom.com/coupons/browse) to see which inserts you can safely toss. Once an insert is no longer listed on his page, all the coupons it contains are expired.

Now instead of clipping out all the coupons when you receive them, you clip only the coupons you need before heading out to the store.

When you're writing out your list, you can see what insert contained a particular coupon by looking in national coupon databases. The two biggest here are:

- Coupon Tom—coupontom.com

- Hot Coupon World—www.hotcouponworld.com/forums/coupon.php

Each also lets you search for expired coupons, if you have local stores that accept these up to a certain date. Hot Coupon World is more thorough, but a bit more overwhelming, since they include tearpads, hangtags, brochures, and other types of coupons, not just inserts. Use the drop-down menu at the top of the search form to limit the search to inserts if you're just looking for coupons by date.

HEADS-UP

Since different areas of the country receive different coupons and coupon values, you will often find a coupon listed in one of these databases that is not actually available in the inserts from your local paper, or yours will be lower value. If your local sale runs for a while, you can consider picking up the regional or higher value coupons from a clipper or from eBay.

We'll talk more in Chapter 16 about planning your shopping trips, but the clip-free method lets you just snip the coupons you need right before you go to the store.

The Binder Method

Some people do prefer to use a coupon binder to organize all of their clipped coupons. The advantage of this system is that it keeps insert coupons and all your other coupons together, so that you can see at a glance what you have.

The main disadvantage is that maintaining a binder is much more time consuming than the clip-free method. Clipping the coupons from one paper takes long enough; clipping and filing all the coupons from multiple weekly papers, booklets, blinkies, and more takes much, much longer.

Look for a sturdy zipper binder to corral your coupons. The best time to buy these is during the back-to-school clearance sales in September. Add some plastic baseball card inserts—which you can find at stores like Target or Walmart or at sites like the2buds.com—to house your coupons so you can see them. Then simply file your clipped coupons alphabetically, by brand, by aisle of the store, or whatever works for you.

The Hybrid Method

Many people (myself included!) use some combination of the clipless and binder methods. You might, for instance, keep Sunday inserts intact in an accordion folder and keep booklets together in a box, but file your clipped Internet, tearpad, and blinkie coupons alphabetically in a binder or file box.

Over time, you'll see which method works best for you and the way you shop.

Bringing Coupons to the Store

Most people don't care to lug around a huge binder (or two!) while shopping. It's easier to pull just the coupons you need for your shopping trip and bring those with you to the store. Throw them in an envelope, clip them together, or get a little checkbook-size coupon wallet that fits inside your purse.

> **TIPS AND TRICKS**
>
> Know your stores' policies. Some let you redeem coupons off your receipts for 30 or 60 days after purchase, so you can pick up clearance finds or sale items even if you don't have your coupons with you. Just bring your receipt back in with the coupons and get the cash back.

Some people do like to bring their binder along so that they have their coupons with them in case of an unexpected sale or clearance find. If you like to be prepared, look for a zipper binder with a carry strap for travel.

You can get fancy and purchase custom-made binder totes at sites like the Coupon Clutch (couponclutch.com) but this isn't necessary. Especially when you're first getting started, don't go overboard buying organizational supplies. The idea here is to save money, and you'll want to see what process works for you before investing any real dollars into it. Your coupons will work just as well when you pull them out of a repurposed envelope.

The Least You Need to Know

- Think outside the box and beyond one Sunday paper when acquiring coupons.
- Swap and share—your unwanted coupons are another's treasure, and vice versa.
- Organize however works for you: folders, binders, box, envelopes, it doesn't matter as long as you can find things.

Blogs and Forums

In This Chapter

- The power of online couponing communities
- Couponing blogs for local and national deals
- Couponing forums for fast-moving discussions
- Using social media sites to keep up

You've picked a great time to start couponing! Online forums and blogs let us share information, trade coupons, and keep up with deals. You don't have to figure out the best deals and coupon match-ups for your local store ads all by yourself, and you don't have to jump around to every daily deals and online shopping site looking for the best sales. Let others help out.

This chapter talks about choosing blogs and forums to follow that will help you spot deals and cut down on your planning and preparation time.

Couponing and Online Communities

As couponing becomes more and more popular, lots of blogs, forums, Facebook pages, and other online resources have emerged. It can be hard to wade through all the options and find the best places for your own needs, but finding your online couponing home is important to maximizing your coupon savings.

We each prefer to receive our information in different ways. Some people are Facebook junkies, some love Twitter, and some like e-mail, while others love the back-and-forth conversations on forums. Luckily, you'll find information and community no matter where you hang out online. Pick whichever method (or methods) fits your preferences, and don't feel compelled to read blogs, or follow forums, or hang out on Facebook if it's not a good fit for you.

Blogs

Blogs are the best way to get started with couponing, since many clearly spell out the best deals at both local stores and national chains. You'll want, at the very least, to find a blogger in your local area who does weekly coupon *matchups* for your local stores.

DEFINITION

Matchups on couponing blogs literally match up sales and deals at local and national chains with the current coupons that go along with them. These matchups detail which coupon insert, booklet, or blinkie contains a matching coupon, or link directly to a coupon you can print out and bring to the store.

Using these matchups lets you go with the clip-free method of organizing coupons, and cuts down tremendously on the time it takes to plan and prepare for your shopping trips.

Blogs keep you updated on local and national coupon matchups and deals.

Some blogs focus primarily on one store, and you can use these if you have a preferred shopping location. These include …

- www.iheartcvs.com for CVS deals.
- www.iheartthemart.com for Walmart deals.
- www.iheartwags.com for Walgreens deals.
- meijermadness.com for Meijer deals.
- www.totallytarget.com for Target deals.
- wildforwags.com for Walgreens deals.

Most blogs, though, cover multiple couponing and sales at both local and national store chains as well as online deals and coupon codes.

How Blogs Work

Blogs are simply a special type of website where new content (or posts) always shows up at the top in reverse chronological order. You always see the newest deals and matchups, so blogs are a great way to keep up with current sales and coupons.

The content on blogs generally comes from individuals or from small groups of people. Only those who run the blog are permitted to post, or to add new content to the blog. Some are very high volume, containing 20–30 new posts a day. Others are much slower and might only contain a post or two each day. Again, find your own comfort level here.

Most blogs offer multiple ways to subscribe to new content. You can sign up for a daily e-mail that contains everything posted during the last 24 hours in one message. This is often less overwhelming for new couponers. The disadvantage here is that many online deals and printable coupons are time sensitive, so by the time you receive the e-mail you have already missed out on some things.

You can also subscribe to blogs via Facebook, Twitter, or RSS (Real Simple Syndication). RSS allows you to subscribe to blogs and other sites to see new content in an RSS reader or site like My Yahoo! as it is posted.

TIPS AND TRICKS

Use an RSS reader such as Google Reader (google.com/reader) or a site like My Yahoo! (my.yahoo.com) to add, organize, and read subscriptions to blogs and other websites. Look for a little orange RSS button on websites. This lets you access the RSS feed and add the subscription.

Since Facebook, Twitter, and RSS all let you see content almost as soon as it is posted, these are better choices than daily e-mails for keeping up with high-volume blogs and time-sensitive deals and coupons.

Finding Blogs

You can sometimes find the main coupon bloggers in your area just by Googling "[*name of local store*] deals"—especially if you live near large regional chains.

Lists of coupon bloggers online can also help you get started, although these are nowhere near comprehensive. BeCentsAble's Grocery Gathering (www.becentsable.net/store-deals) lists frugal bloggers by state, while Bargain Briana hosts a similar Frugal Map (thefrugalmap.bargainbriana.com/the-frugal-map).

Once you start reading a blog or two in your area, they can help you find additional blogs to follow. On the blog home pages check their right-hand sidebars for lists of links to other couponing and frugality blogs that they like. You will also see them crediting other bloggers for deals in their posts, so click through to see whom coupon bloggers read themselves!

In major metropolitan and suburban areas, you generally have a choice among several bloggers. Pick the one or ones that seem most comprehensive and that you enjoy reading. Since blogs are run by individuals or small teams, they each have their own voice and personality. While they may cover most of the same deals, one will be a better fit for the way you shop or the way you like to read your info.

Add Your Input

Most blogs allow you to comment, or add your input to individual posts. Look at the bottom of each post, and you'll see a link to add a comment or to view comments. Click and you'll see others' comments plus a box to add your own. Realize that your comments can be read by anyone who visits that blog, so refrain from posting personal information or anything you don't want the whole world to see.

COUPON QUIPS

On most blogs, visitors' first comments are held for moderation. Just like you get "spam" messages in your e-mail box, blogs are susceptible to comment spam, so your comment will have to be manually approved. Once you've been approved, future comments generally go through without moderation. So if you comment but don't see it appear right away, don't panic.

If you have a question about a deal, or have found a new coupon or matchup or sale, this is a great place to add your voice. Bloggers love receiving comments, and the more people who contribute, the more the entire community surrounding that blog benefits.

Bloggers get their information from multiple resources, and one main source is their own readers—the more pairs of eyes searching out the deals, the better. If you're unsure about commenting publicly, you can also e-mail the blogger directly or contact her from the form on her site (usually found on a "contact" or "about" page in the top menu bar).

Forums

Forums are often best for more advanced couponers. They're fast moving, and the specific information about a deal often gets buried in a lot of chit-chat and discussion. You'll need to have patience and persistence to participate.

You can choose from both large national forums and smaller local forums. National forums generally include subforums for various stores and topics, helping you focus on areas of interest and find information more quickly.

The main national couponing forums include:

- FatWallet—www.fatwallet.com
- A Full Cup—www.afullcup.com
- Hot Coupon World—www.hotcouponworld.com
- Slickdeals—slickdeals.net
- WeUseCoupons—www.weusecoupons.com

National forums are a fantastic resource for online deals and deals at major national chains. Since they pull information from people all over the country, they often contain posts on deals that have not yet hit the blogs. Forums are also a great place to trade coupons.

How Forums Work

While the content on blogs is generally maintained by one person or a small team of people, the content on forums is mainly generated by each forum's members. Anyone who signs up can post new content or reply to others' posts, although, as with blogs, your first effort may be held for moderation before it appears, to ensure you're not a spammer.

Forums basically work like ongoing conversations about different topics. On couponing and deals forums, people talk about couponing and deals topics. Forums provide members with a way to share information with each other, and the site provides the record of that ongoing conversation.

Rather than new content always appearing at the top of the page, as on blogs, new replies appear either at the first or last page of a topic (depending on how the forum software is set up). Forums are organized into smaller subtopics and then into specific conversations within those topics.

So a national forum might, for example, have a section for grocery stores, then within that a section for Kroger, then within that various individual topics such as "deals this week" or "Catalina deals" or "unadvertised specials." Drill down to the specific topic of interest to find the information you're looking for or topic you wish to participate in.

Finding Forums

You can choose to join one of the large national forums previously listed. The main advantage of these is that they are huge, so you will find the largest quantity of deals. The main disadvantage also is that they are huge, so it's easy to get lost and hard to find specific information.

You can sometimes find local forums the same way you find local blogs. Google search "[*name of your store*] forum."

Add Your Input

Since forum content comes directly from users, adding your voice to forums is even more important than adding your comments to blogs. Some even have minimum participation requirements, making users post monthly or so in order to maintain their membership.

Communities are only as strong as their people. *Newbies* to forums and other online communities often hang back, thinking that they don't have anything to contribute to an established online community. Again, these communities flourish because of the power of many pairs of eyes; the more people out there looking for deals and matching up the coupons, the better everyone fares.

DEFINITION

New forum members and new couponers are often referred to as **newbies.** This isn't meant to be insulting, but a reminder that all of us were new at some point.

Newbies often spot hidden deals that more experienced couponers overlook, simply because they buy items that veteran couponers don't. When your stockpile is less built up, you might buy an item that doesn't seem to be on sale—but has a surprise Catalina deal attached. You might be shopping at a store that veterans skip because it has fewer sales this week—but spot an amazing cart full of clearance items.

When you have a real deal to contribute, be sure to speak up. That's how you give back and how you build up a good online reputation. You'll need to develop a thick skin, though, anytime you post online. Since anyone can participate in online communities, you'll find both welcoming and cranky members—just as you do in any real life community.

However you also want to make sure not to post irrelevant content or to ask questions that have already been answered. Forums usually have FAQs (Frequently Asked Questions) posted for new members. Read these before posting to see if your question has been answered, scroll through the topic, or thread, to see if someone has already posted the same information, and use the search function to see if you can locate the info or answer.

Repeated questions or posts are a common pet peeve on forums, and you might not get a pleasant response. Some forums are unmoderated, meaning anything goes, and some are only lightly moderated. Forums are made up of people, so you'll get the same mix as in real life—some are pleasant, some are helpful, and some are outright angry or rude. Be prepared to grow a thick skin anytime you put yourself out there online.

Facebook

Facebook isn't just for friends anymore. We talked way back in Chapter 3 about "liking" brands and companies on Facebook so that you can print high-value coupons for fans. You can also "like" blogs and other coupon sites on Facebook, so that the deals they post show up in your news feed and you see these whenever you log on to Facebook.

Other coupon sites solely use Facebook pages rather than maintain a separate blog. Here your only option will be to like them on Facebook and get their deals that way.

Twitter

Most coupon blogs now have associated Twitter feeds, where the headline to each new post comes through almost as soon as it is posted. This is a great way to keep up with new coupons and deals. When you follow several blogs, instead of having to go back to their sites to see what's new, simply leave Twitter open and watch the deals come in.

Since so many more people are couponing now, printable coupons tend to hit their limits quickly and online deals tend to sell out quickly. Don't miss out: stay on top of new coupons and deals by adding several local bloggers to your Twitter feed.

How Twitter Works

To use Twitter, you'll need to create an account on the site. You can then subscribe to, or "follow," other Twitter accounts. All of their Twitter comments, or tweets, then show up on your Twitter home page as they are posted.

Finding Twitter Feeds

Check your favorite blogs for a link to their Twitter feeds—which may say Twitter, or may just picture a little blue bird. Most automatically feed their posts to Twitter, which means you'll see all the content come through there as soon as it is posted. Many also tweet timely or small deals that never make it through to the blog itself.

The Least You Need to Know

- Pick one or more online couponing communities as your online coupon home.
- Choose to participate—and if you have a deal, share; if you have a question, ask.
- Subscribe to information on coupons and deals so that it comes right to you—save your time and make it easy.

Planning Your Shopping Trips

In This Chapter

- Plan out your trip to avoid surprises at the register
- Plan to stock up seasonally
- Know the policies at different stores

You now have all the tools you need to get going: You know where to find coupons, where to print coupons, and how to acquire multiple coupons. You know how to combine coupons with sale prices and money-back offers. And you know where to find online info on all the deals.

Let's put it all together and learn how to combine these strategies at different stores. This chapter talks about the best ways to plan your shopping trips for maximum savings.

Plot a Productive Trip

Once you know the different strategies for couponing at the store, your savings really boil down to how well you plan out your trips. Effective couponing requires planning: you can't just pop by the store and buy whatever you want, whenever you want. That's an easy way to blow all of your savings.

Since sales go in cycles, and coupons come and go, you'll need to stock up whenever you can get the lowest price by combining sales and coupons. You can buy most of the things you want over time; you just need to time your purchases and match your coupons up with sales.

Avoid impulse buys and blowing your budget on full-price items by always making up a list before you go to the store. Know what you are going to buy, how much each item costs, what coupons you are going to use, and what you expect to pay at the register.

If you do add items to your list while you're in the store, account for those and know approximately what you should be paying at checkout. Even small impulse items add up—a dollar here, two dollars there—and that's how we end up with hundreds of dollars in groceries with little to show for it.

> **COUPON QUIPS**
>
> Having a rough total in mind before you get to the register also helps prevent you from being overcharged, which happens often, unfortunately. If something seems fishy, check your receipts and get any overcharges corrected before you leave the store. Some grocery stores have a policy that you get an item *free* if it rings wrong at the register, so stop by the service desk to get your complete refund.

Make your lists using a mobile app like GroceryIQ, or jot them down on slips of paper, whatever works best for you. I like to make mine in rough order by store layout so that I don't forget anything in the store.

Then just clip, print, or load the coupons you intend to use on that particular trip. Clip them to your list or stick them in an envelope, and you're off and ready to go!

Start Online

While you want to plan effectively, you also don't want to devote your whole life to couponing—you have other things to do. Just as we don't want to cross the line from stockpiling to hoarding, we don't want to cross the line from organized to obsessive. Couponing is a part of your life, not your entire life.

Luckily, blogs and other online resources cut down the amount of time you need to devote to planning. Plan to take about half an hour before a weekly shopping trip to browse the matchups at your favorite blog or forum, make your list, and cut your coupons. It might take you a bit longer when you're just getting started and getting used to the process, but you'll get faster as you go.

If you plan to visit more than one store to cherry pick the best deals, you'll want to spend a bit more time planning your trips. Like anything else, we can choose how much time and effort we want to put into couponing.

TIPS AND TRICKS

Many coupon blogs have a "create shopping list" function that lets you check off the items you want to add from their matchups. Others have a "print-friendly" function that lets you select sections of their matchup posts to print without graphics and sidebars. Use these functions to print shopping lists with coupon info attached.

As you read your favorite blogs, forums, Facebook pages, and other websites throughout the week, make a note of any in-store deals that strike your fancy. Some people copy and paste these into a Word document, or paste them into an e-mail to themselves that they can pull up on their smartphone in the store, while some prefer to print them out. Over time, you'll find out what works best for you.

Browse the Circulars

When you get your Sunday paper or receive your local store circulars in the mail each week, take a few minutes to browse through the flyers yourself. Even though your local coupon bloggers will cover the major sales circulars in their matchups, we all have different shopping patterns and different ideas of what makes a good deal.

You might spot a sale that makes you happy, but that someone else will miss. A blogger who doesn't buy organic foods, for instance, might miss an organic sale; one who doesn't drink alcohol might miss a deal on your favorite beer.

Coupon bloggers also don't often cover smaller chains or rural stores, which means you can't always rely solely on the deals put together by others. Your small local store, produce store, or ethnic market might be running a sale better than any major chains this week, but you'll have to do those matchups yourself.

As you go through the ad and make note of the sale items that look good to you, check online coupon databases like Hot Coupon World and Coupon Tom for insert and printable coupons that match up with them. When deciding which items to stock up on, look at the sale prices, whether your family is running low, and what coupons are available.

Plan Seasonal Stock-Ups

While grocery sales are cyclical and most items hit low price points every 3 months or so, you can also count on a number of seasonal sales. Some items hit their very lowest price point just once a year.

> **COUPON QUIPS**
>
> When it comes to seasonal stock-up items, you want to stock up for longer than the normal 10–12 week cycle. Luckily, many have long expiration dates or can be frozen for some time. Every Fourth of July, I stock up on name-brand hot dogs for $.49 or less a package, and just pull them out of the freezer as needed the rest of the year. Every August, we pick up free pens and near-free paper to stock our home office for a year. Every November, we pick up a couple of extra hams to freeze for a nice family dinner later in the year.

These yearly sales often coincide with holidays or clearance sales after holidays, and sometimes with events like National Dairy Month or National Frozen Food Month. (Yes, really—we have national months for foods!)

Months to Stock Up on Various Items

Month	Event	Examples of Items
January	post-holiday	Gift wrap, toys, clothes
February	Valentine's Day	Candy
March	Frozen Food month	Frozen veggies, ice cream
April	Easter, Passover	Candy, hams, Kosher items
May	Memorial Day	Hot dogs, soda
June	Dairy Month	Yogurt, butter, sour cream
July	Independence Day	Hot dogs, soda
August	back-to-school	Pens, pencils, paper
September	Labor Day	Soda, summer clearance
October	Halloween	Candy
November	Thanksgiving	Flour, sugar, turkeys
December	Christmas, Chanukah, Kwanzaa	Hams, electronics, toys

Think of ways to stock up on seasonal produce items as well. You can freeze berries, peppers, and other cheap summer produce for use throughout the winter months. Flash freeze them in a single layer on a cookie sheet, then store in freezer bags once frozen—this prevents them from freezing in clumps.

Allow for Surprises

You can plan all day, but you never know quite what you'll find when you go to the store. You want to leave allowances in your budget for unexpected clearance items, and you want to leave flexibility in your plans for unexpected empty shelves at the store.

Clean Up on Clearance

Some surprises are happy. On a recent trip to a local grocery boneless-skinless chicken breasts were marked $1.99/lb.—and they all had 30 percent off stickers! Had I planned to buy chicken that day? No. Did I buy chicken? At $1.39 a pound for organic meat, heck yes!

Allow room in your budget for happy surprises that help you build or replenish your stockpile. Yes, I bought $15 worth of chicken that day, but two thirds of it went straight into the freezer. The next week, none of my local stores had chicken on sale, but I just shopped from my freezer and planned out poultry dinners anyway. Going over my planned spending one week allowed me to spend less the next; it all evens out over time.

> **HEADS-UP**
>
> Know the difference between clearance stock-ups and impulse buys. The key here: is this an item your family needs and will use before it expires? If something's a great price but you don't need it, let it go. There will always be another deal.

Many stores will let you bring in coupons and redeem them off your receipt later, if you don't have them along when you spot a random clearance deal. (We'll talk a bit later in this chapter about knowing your store's policies.)

You also can stock up seasonally on clearance clothing and toys. Look for clearance winter items in spring, clearance summer items in fall. Stores like Old Navy run biannual 50 percent off sales on clearance prices, and Target runs a 75 percent off toy clearance mid-January and mid-July. Buy ahead, because clearance winter clothes purchased a size up will be perfect for when the kids are back in school late fall, and clearance toys can stock your birthday closet for parties throughout the year.

Go to Plan B

Some surprises are less happy. You might have carefully planned a scenario that combines coupons with store sales and a money-back Catalina offer, but then get to the store to find that someone else has already cleared the shelf. You might find that a fantastic advertised price was a typo, and the store has signs up apologizing for the misprint, but too bad, so sad. You might find that the rock-bottom fruit you planned to stock up on is moldy and unappetizing.

Now what?

If something is out of stock, always ask for a rain check. This might make for an even better deal later, if a higher-value coupon comes out before the rain check expires. Unfortunately, most stores will not write rain checks with Catalina offers attached—CVS is one exception, as they will write you a rain check that includes the ECB offer.

Also check with your store manager to see when they restock. They might run out of an item, yet get a truck in overnight and have full shelves again by morning; you just hit them at just the wrong time.

> **TIPS AND TRICKS**
>
> Forestall many problems by shopping early. As more and more people are couponing, more and more stores run out of stock on hot items early in a sale. Whenever possible, shop on the day a sale begins.

On a multi-item Catalina, Extra Bucks, or Register Rewards offer, it's useful to have an alternative plan in mind before you go to the store. If item A is out of stock, will you be able to substitute item B for a similar deal?

And if you planned to stock up but the item is out of stock or un-appealing, try again later in the week or wait for another sale or another store. There will always be another deal.

Preorder

If you do plan to stock up heavily during a fantastic sale, talk to your store manager and see if they'll let you preorder products. This ensures that you get your items, and also leaves stock on the shelf for other customers. Only do this if you plan to buy in quantity—think cases here, not ones and twos.

If you do preorder items, be sure to pick them up and pay for them. Stores that get stuck with unsold stock after a sale ends because you happened to change your mind won't be too happy with you.

Know Your Store's Policies

In order to plan, you need to know your local store's coupon policy. These can vary wildly from store to store: Some will take competitor coupons; some will not. Some allow two coupons on a buy-one-get-one free sale; some will not. Some will take manufacturer coupons that show other stores' logos; some will not. Some will give overage if the face value of the coupon is more than the item's price; some will not. You don't want to get shot down at the register or end up paying more than expected because you didn't know the rules.

Most grocery stores and drugstores post their coupon policies prominently on their websites, and the policy should also be available at the customer service desk at each store. If you can't find the policy on your local store's site, do a quick Google search for "[*name of store*] coupon policy."

HEADS-UP

Sometimes cashiers are not well trained in their own store's policies. Especially if you have a less coupon-friendly store, print out their policy and carry it with you in case of problems. Write the corporate customer service number on your printed copy in case you need to give them a call.

Policies also change over time, so check in every once in a while to be sure your copy remains current.

Doubling Policies

You'll also need to know your store's policy on doubling coupons, especially as these have been changing recently. In some areas of the country, some grocery stores double the face value of manufacturer coupons. At these stores a $.25 coupon, for instance, would actually give you $.50 off an item.

A few regional chains, such as Albertsons in the Pacific Northwest, don't double as a general rule but periodically publish special in-ad doubler coupons. These are typically limited to two or four doubled coupons per transaction (or day), and you have to choose the manufacturer coupons you want doubled with your in-ad doubler.

Other stores require a minimum purchase and only double a certain number of coupons. For example, you might only be allowed to double five coupons with a minimum $25 purchase.

Before you get to the register, you'll also want to know: What face value will the store double up to? Some double coupons up to $.50, some up to $1. How many "like" coupons will they double? Many will only double four of the same manufacturer coupon per transaction. Will their registers automatically double coupons with "do not double" wording?

Some stores only give credit up to a certain dollar amount for doubled coupons. For example, if your store only gives double credit up to $1, a $.50 coupon doubles to $1—but a $.75 coupon also doubles to $1, not to $1.50.

Lastly, stores generally double only up to an item's price. So if you have a $.75 coupon for a $1.25 item, it will double to $1.25 rather than $1.50—you won't get the overage.

HEADS-UP

Some stores, run occasional special double events. Kmart, for instance, sometimes doubles coupons up to $.99 for Shop Your Way Rewards members. These events often have restrictions, such as five doubled coupons per day with a minimum $25 purchase, so you'll have to decide if it's worth your while to participate.

Doubled coupons can be very valuable, and often get you items for free. If an item is on sale for $1 and you have a $.50 coupon, it's yours for free. This is why you'll see many of the couponers on TV picking up items like Yakisoba noodle bowls, which are almost always free after doubled coupon. A $.50 Starkist tuna pouch coupon doubles to make the pouches free when they go on sale for $1.

Doubles are another reason why coupon values vary regionally. Areas in which some stores double coupons under $1, for example, might see a $1/2 coupon in their coupon inserts to prevent doubling, while areas that don't double might receive a $.50 or $.55/1 coupon for the same product. This is another time to look for coupons on eBay or from a clipper: another region's coupons can make items at your stores free.

Price Matching Policies

Stores that match the prices in local competitors' ads, such as Target and Walmart, also have specific price match policies you'll need to be aware of. Again, look on the store's website or do a Google search to find their particular policy.

Stores that do price match generally only price match local stores, and local may be defined differently by each store. They will not price match warehouse clubs, and Target won't price match loyalty card pricing—which leaves out many grocery store chains. They also only price match identical items, so if they only carry a different size or brand, you're out of luck.

TIPS AND TRICKS

Some stores now offer electronic price matching: load a price match from a local competitor onto your store loyalty card, and the item will ring up at that price at the register. In Illinois, for example, Dominick's "Deal Match" (dealmatch.dominicks.com) lets shoppers load their choices from a short list of preselected price matches from a local grocery store and Target.

Target has some more special price match rules. You need to price match at the service desk rather than at the register. They'll also apply any Target store coupons before the price match, meaning that you can't actually use a price match with store coupons to get a better deal.

Restrictions aside, price matching can help cut down on the number of trips you need to make, which is a bonus in a time of sky-high gas prices. You can also collect produce ads from local markets and price match produce prices, letting you get great deals without having to bop around to multiple small markets.

The Least You Need to Know

- Plan to save, and save the plan; make a list but leave room for some flexibility at the store.
- Stock up on sale items, both on cyclical sales every few weeks and seasonally across the year.
- Know before you go—learn your stores' policies on everything from doubles to price matching.

Couponing for Your Priorities

In This Chapter

- A dollar saved here, a dollar to use there
- Find coupons for specialty products online and from the manufacturer
- Change your strategies to match the size of your family and your location

You all know the popular myth that couponing only works on huge quantities of unhealthy, overly processed food. But couponing strategies can help us save—no matter our family's priorities, size, and needs. We can all coupon the best way for our family. You don't have to keep up with the coupon Joneses, and you don't have to get everything for free: saving is saving.

This chapter outlines some of the best strategies for shifting your dollars toward your own priorities, giving both general suggestions and specific advice for specific needs.

Shifting Your Dollars

A few general strategies will help you shift your dollars so that you can use them on your priorities, no matter your diet or your family's needs. Whether you choose to eat organic, need to follow a gluten-free diet, or just want to add in more produce and whole foods, saving in one or more other areas frees up the budget you need to fund your priorities.

Free Drugstore Finds

When you follow a special diet or are looking to eat healthier, you may not want to stock up on many of the processed grocery store items (salty noodle bowls, candy, etc.) that we often can get for free with coupons. However, you can instead choose to focus your couponing efforts where they'll make the most difference in your budget.

Any time we can purchase everyday items with coupons rather than with cash, that opens up additional money in our budgets for different priorities. Think about what you've been spending on everyday necessities like health and beauty items, and think about what you could otherwise do with that money.

> **COUPON QUIPS**
>
> You can choose organic for free at the drugstore, too! In the past couple of months alone, I've picked up Honest Tea for better than free after printable coupons and ECB at CVS, and have scored free organic eos lip balm at Walgreens.

We talked in Chapters 7 and 8 about saving at the drugstore and stacking up your savings. When you bring home drugstore items for free or better than free, the funds that otherwise would have been spent on toothpaste, shampoo, ibuprofen, and feminine hygiene products can instead go towards organic milk, gluten-free bread, or veggie burgers.

Catalina Madness

Catalinas can be a couponer's best friend. Since these are money-back coupons good for almost anything else in the store, you can use them to buy your produce, meat, or organic milk. It's create-your-own coupon time!

When you combine coupons with sales to get a great price on Catalina-producing items, then these on-your-next-order coupons you get back are a bonus. It's better for your budget to use Monopoly money rather than actual hard-earned cash to buy items it's hard to find coupons for.

Owning Overage

Instead of confining your grocery shopping to pricey specialty stores like Whole Foods, strategically shift some of your trips over to everyday stores like Walmart. Walmart gives overage for coupons with a face value higher than a product's price, which is a great way to give to others while also stocking up on your own family's needs (especially if you have a Walmart Supercenter near you!).

Here's an example: Similac releases a manufacturer coupon in a newspaper insert good for $5 off any Similac item. At Walmart, some of the Similac ready-to-feed bottles of formula sell for as little as $3.74. This means that, for each bottle of formula you purchase with a $5 coupon, you earn $1.26 towards the other items in your order.

So you look around the store, and find that Cascadian Farms organic frozen vegetables sell for $2.48—and you're also armed with a $.75/1 Cascadian Farms coupon you've printed from Coupons.com.

$2.48 Cascadian Farms veggies
+$3.74 formula

$6.22

-$.75 veggies coupon
-$5.00 formula coupon

$.52 for both veggies and formula

If you just bought Cascadian Farms and used the $.75 coupon, you'd pay $1.74 for your organic veggies. But if you throw in a bottle of formula and use the $5 coupon as well, you end up paying just $.52 for both.

Don't need formula, or whatever else you're buying for overage this week? Donate your Similac to your local food pantry, crisis pregnancy center, or church, feast on the veggies, and do well by doing good. There's always someone who can use the items you can't; excess purchases will never go to waste.

Finding Specialty Coupons

Smaller natural, organic, and allergen-free companies generally can't afford to blow their budgets by issuing large quantities of coupons in the Sunday newspaper inserts, especially knowing that most people will just toss these. Instead, they release their coupons in specialty stores or online.

Look for national booklets like the monthly *Mambo Sprouts* or *Healthy Clippings* at health food stores or Whole Foods, and keep an eye out for coupons whenever visiting these stores, just like you do in "regular" grocery stores. Beyond the store, though, you can find many more coupons by digging a little more deeply.

Specialty Coupon Sites

Several sites are devoted entirely to coupons for organic, natural, and gluten-free products. At Mambo Sprouts (www.mambosprouts.com), for instance, you can often find printable coupons for brands like Organic Valley, San-J, and Crunchmaster.

Mambo Sprouts tends to add a larger new batch of coupons at the beginning of each month, then randomly adds a few here and there throughout the rest of the month.

Mambo Sprouts provides coupons for natural, gluten-free, and organic products.

At HealthESavers (healthesavers.com), find additional printable coupons for natural brands and nutritional supplements. They have fewer coupons, but you can also sign up for their e-mail newsletter for additional alerts.

If you shop Whole Foods, you can also print many of their Whole Deal store coupons online (wholefoodsmarket.com/coupons). Some Whole Foods let you stack manufacturer and store coupons—which can lead to fantastic savings, and sometimes make items free—while others do not. Check with your local store for their policy.

Beyond the specialty sites, also check the big general coupon sites, which often contain coupons for organic, natural, and gluten-free items. Be sure to visit at the beginning of each month, because these limited print coupons get snatched up quickly.

Manufacturer Websites

Identify the products you buy most often, and visit the manufacturer's website for each. See if they have a coupons, offers, or promotions page, and sign up for their e-mail newsletter and Facebook fan page. Companies ranging from Wholly (guacamole) to Stonyfield Farm are fantastic about releasing regular coupons on their sites, on their Facebook pages, and via e-mail.

> **COUPON QUIPS**
>
> Even items we don't tend to think of as branded, like produce and meat, often really are: Driscoll's offers berry coupons on their website; Fresh Express has released salad coupons on their Facebook page. Gold'n Plump chicken regularly offers printables on their site; Laura's Lean Beef gives you coupons when you sign up for e-mail. Check brand websites for whole foods, not just processed products.

Rather than issuing paper coupons, many companies prefer to keep it in the family and offer printable coupons as rewards to their newsletter subscribers or Facebook fans.

Contact the Manufacturer

If you've exhausted all the usual sources for coupons, contact the company directly. Many of these companies are smaller and more eager to interact with fans, so a simple plea for coupons can often pay off well.

Shopping Online

You will also want to look online for deals on items that are often very expensive in store. Amazon is a fantastic resource for organic and gluten-free products in particular, and when you combine Subscribe & Save with monthly coupon codes you often can get these items shipped to your door for less than you can find them for in local stores.

Couponing for Special Diets

So now that we've talked about general strategies for saving on your priorities, let's talk some specific tips for particular diets.

Organic Diets

First, decide on your organic priorities. Is it important that all your produce be organic, or just the items that tend to be most highly contaminated with pesticides? Is it more important to you to eat organic, or to eat locally? Is it important that all your dairy products be organic, or just milk? Is it important that all your meat be organic, or is it sufficient if it's natural and nitrate-free?

> **TIPS AND TRICKS**
>
> The Environmental Working Group (ewg.org/foodnews) issues a yearly list of the "dirty dozen" most contaminated produce items, as well as the "clean fifteen" that are safest to purchase conventionally.

Making some choices about your organic priorities can help you save. You might always buy organic strawberries, apples, and celery, which are some of the most commonly pesticide-contaminated items, but might choose always to buy conventional onions and corn, which are among the "cleanest" produce items. Save your organic dollars for the worst offenders.

Also, look beyond the grocery store for your produce. Visit farmers' markets, especially in areas with a long growing season. This also lets you shop locally and seasonally. Another alternative in many areas is joining a CSA (Community Supported Agriculture). Here, you buy into a share of the products from a local farm, and receive fresh, local, seasonal produce throughout the growing season.

In a CSA, though, be sure to see what you're signing up for. Many CSAs just include veggie boxes, but others might include fruit, eggs, and more. CSAs allow you to get to know who is growing your food and about their practices, and ensures that you have a steady supply of local produce throughout the season in your area. However, with a CSA, you have to take what you get and what's in season. If your family is picky, you'll need to branch out and learn to cook with some unfamiliar vegetables.

Use Local Harvest (www.localharvest.org) to locate CSAs, farmers' markets, farms, and other places to buy local produce and meat near you. This allows you to get to know the practices of the farmers who grow your food, and how acceptable they are to you.

When you shop at your local grocery stores, branch out beyond Whole Foods. You can often find the same items for less at general grocery stores, Target, or Walmart, so save your trips to specialty stores for items you can't find elsewhere or to stock up on sale items, just as you do at other high/low grocery stores. If you have a Trader Joe's in your area, they're a great resource for everyday low prices on organic and natural products (and they do take coupons, although most of their items are private label). Warehouse clubs can be a surprisingly good choice for cage-free eggs and bulk organic produce.

Also, watch for organic deals on deal-of-the-day sites. Groupon, for instance, has offered vouchers for organic and natural sites like Abe's Market (www.abesmarket.com). Groupon and sites like LivingSocial and FamilyFinds have offered vouchers for half-price delivery boxes of organic produce or local deliveries of grass-fed beef. Even if you only take advantage of that one-time deal, that's a week's worth of organic veggies or local humanely treated meats for half the price.

Sites like Organic Deals (www.organicdeals.com) and Healthy Life Deals (www.healthylifedeals.com) can help you track both online and in-store deals on organic products.

Allergen-Free Diets

Allergen-free shoppers can use many of the same strategies as organic shoppers to locate coupons and deals. Print gluten-free and lactose-free coupons on sites like Mambo Sprouts, and sign up with manufacturers to print coupons from their websites and e-mail lists. Stalk Amazon.com for deals on specialty products, and watch the deal-of-the-day sites for vouchers.

COUPON QUIPS

Think outside the box—literally! Manufacturers try to get us to think we need specialty foods for special diets. You can often save more with coupons and sales on allergen-free regular foods (such as gluten-free Chex cereals) rather than on pricey items made specifically for specialty diets.

Also, think about buying the ingredients for your own allergen-free recipes rather than purchasing prepackaged goods. Rather than buying Lactaid milk at three times the price of regular milk, for example, you can purchase a bottle of Lactase drops on Amazon and add them to a gallon of regular milk. Rather than buying a $4 box of gluten-free brownie mix, buy some bulk gluten-free flour and make your own.

Low-Carb Diets

One of the first tips you always hear for saving on groceries is to go meatless at least a couple of nights a week. Alternative protein sources like beans are generally much cheaper, and stretch much further. Well, what can you do if you follow a diet like Atkins, which depends heavily on meat and cheese and eschews those high-carb beans?

First, follow the principles we've been talking about throughout: Stock up when prices are low. Meat hits those rock-bottom prices just like anything else, and you'll also want to watch for clearance and markdowns on close-to-expiration products. Find out when your local stores' meat department marks items down—is there a certain time of day or day of the week you're more likely to find clearance items?

Chat with your butcher and get to know your store's patterns. Stores tend to mark down clearance meats by 50 percent or more, so if you stalk this week's sale items and snatch them up on clearance, that can make for a great per-pound price.

Now, look for alternative protein sources that aren't carb-based. Eggs are Atkins-friendly, and are good for weeks after the sell-by date. Mix it up and have omelets for dinner, or scramble up some breakfast burritos in a low-carb wrap.

Lastly, rebates can be a carnivore's friend. Stalk the liquor department, of all places, for tearpads and hangtags containing rebate forms for "any" poultry, beef, or seafood. Some may also require the purchase of the alcohol, but sometimes you'll see "no beer purchase required" or "purchase of wine not required" generic rebate forms.

Vegetarian and Vegan Diets

On the other end of the spectrum, vegetarians and vegans also have particular couponing needs—but you inherently spend less at the store if you cut out meat. Start by following specialty blogs and sites like the Vegan Coupons Facebook page (facebook.com/vegancoupons).

Vegetarians and vegans can follow many of the same strategies as those shopping for organic items: Shop farmers' markets, sign up for CSAs, and watch Amazon for the deals. And as with allergen-free diets, you'll often save by making your own veggie burgers and other meat alternatives, rather than buying processed specialty foods.

Couponing for Small Families and in Rural Areas

When you're miles from the nearest store, it makes less sense to cherry-pick the deals, and you need to adapt your shopping strategies to your location. When you're shopping for one or two rather than a family, your buying patterns will be different, and buying in the quantities necessary for maximum savings becomes impractical. But it's possible to save, no matter your needs and circumstances.

Rural Areas

How do you coupon when you have few stores near you? Given our sky-high gas prices lately, you may not want to shop around at different stores, or may grocery shop only biweekly or monthly. You will miss deals this way, but you also automatically curb the impulse buys that can pile up with smaller trips to the store.

You'll also want to plan those fewer trips strategically. While you'll have less opportunity to cherry-pick the deals, you'll still want to stock up at low price points—and will want to stock up for longer periods of time. Supplement with delivered grocery items from Amazon, which often has a price advantage over local stores in rural areas with little competition.

For One or Two

The couponing game changes when you have a small family or are buying for one or two. As we've seen, the biggest savings often require buying in quantity. When you're only buying for one, or for a couple, you might not wish to buy or store as many items.

COUPON QUIPS

Be clever about your storage solutions in small spaces. Use under-bed risers to create storage; use built-ins to create storage without looking bulky. You'll usually find more space than you anticipate.

When you don't have storage space for a large stockpile, this also affects the way that you shop. You'll need to be choosier about *which* items you stockpile, and focus on those your family uses most often, plus those you less often find deals on.

However, you do need to shift your thinking a bit. Even if you are shopping for one or two, you can still buy ahead. You might think you only need one or two of a product—but if it's cheaper to buy multiples and they have a long expiration date, why not buy six, even if that will last you six months?

Couponing for Growing Families

On the other end of the spectrum, your shopping patterns and needs inevitably change when you add a new little one into the mix. Those diapers and wipes don't come cheap, and your income may be down as one parent chooses to stay at home or reduce their hours at work. So how do you best save for those baby essentials?

Manufacturer Websites

Start by signing up at every manufacturer website you can think of, from Pampers to Gerber to Similac (even if you're not planning on bottle feeding, as they'll add your name to other lists!). This gives you access to printable coupons, and you'll also receive coupons and samples via postal mail.

TIPS AND TRICKS

If you do choose to use or supplement with formula, formula companies will send formula checks to registered members. These are *not* coupons. They are checks, will have your name on them, and can be stacked with manufacturer coupons for the same item.

Also sign up at store sites like Babies 'R' Us (www.babiesrus.com) and Buy Buy Baby (www.buybuybaby.com), which puts you on their mailing lists for both e-mail and mailed coupons. Create a baby registry at multiple stores as well, which gets you on all their mailing lists for coupons.

Stack the Savings

Drugstores in particular often run on-your-next-order coupon specials on baby items. When you stack these with manufacturer coupons and sales, you can regularly get products like diapers and wipes for 50 percent or less of everyday prices—so stock up on these when you get the chance, just like you'd stock up on food.

Amazon.com

Be sure to join Amazon Mom (www.amazon.com/gp/mom/signup/info) for your three-month 20 percent discount plus free shipping on select diapers and wipes. When you stack this discount with sales, you can often score diapers on Amazon for less than at any local store—shipped directly to your door. If you're an Amazon Prime member, continue those discounts indefinitely.

Toys

With kids comes holidays, birthdays, and more—and toys are expensive! Be sure to sign your kids up for birthday clubs at stores like Toys 'R' Us, since they'll get a free ($1–$5) gift card plus birthday balloon.

But beyond that, clearance sales will be your best friend. Target, for instance, runs a biannual 75 percent off toy clearance in mid-January and mid-July—stock your birthday closet then for the rest of the year.

COUPON QUIPS

Don't mind them used? Check Craigslist, local resale shops, and garage sales for the absolute best toy deals around.

Amazon is your friend here as well. Check their toys clearance section, and stalk their site daily during November to December for amazing holiday toy deals (that often sell out fast).

The Least You Need to Know

- The same strategies help you save no matter your diet or location.
- You don't have to keep up with anyone, nor do you have to get everything for free—saving is still saving.
- Think outside the box when finding both coupons and deals.

Organizing and Donating

Chapter 18

In This Chapter

- Getting organized
- Sorting and donating
- Couponing to stretch your donation dollars

After you have been stockpiling items for a while, you'll find you really need to get organized. You don't want to let items go bad while they're sitting around waiting for you to get around to using them. And you want to make sure you have easy access to your bounty, without letting it take over your life.

Regularly sort through your stockpile to see what's nearing its expiration date. What isn't your family likely to use after all? There's always someone who can make use of what you can't, and it's better to donate your bounty to others than have it sit unused.

This chapter talks about the best ways to organize your stockpile, donate your excess, and use couponing as a tool to share with others.

Organizing Your Stockpile

Once you start couponing, you'll end up with a stockpile of commonly purchased items that you've bought at rock-bottom prices. When you throw items onto shelves and into cupboards willy-nilly, it's easy to lose track of what you have. When you don't know what you have, you buy what you don't need and end up letting items expire.

You don't have to line your entire basement or garage with floor-to-ceiling shelves, but you will want to find storage solutions that fit into your lifestyle, your shopping patterns, and your available space.

> **TIPS AND TRICKS**
>
> Keep similar items together in your stockpile: peanut butter and jelly; jarred spaghetti sauce and pasta. This helps you look through quickly for easy meal ideas from your stash.

When you're organizing your stockpile in different areas around your home, keep similar items together. You might keep all your condiments on one shelf, all your cereal on another. You might keep all your toiletries under your bathroom sink and all your paper items in your linen closet.

If you store the same item in multiple places, it's impossible to know what you have. Keep ongoing track of what you have in stock, to help you plan meals and shopping trips.

Organize on the Cheap

You can pick up a lot of pricey products aimed at helping you organize, everything from can rotators to tiered shelf inserts. (Want some? Try www.ShelfReliance.com or the Container Store—or, visit Bed Bath and Beyond when they release 20 percent off coupons in your local paper.) While these can be pretty and tempting, you don't necessarily need them. A can of soup is the same can of soup, whether you store it in a cardboard box or a custom-made organizer.

Think about alternative homemade solutions to help you organize efficiently. For example, you might use shoeboxes to collect everything from toothpaste to shampoo under your sink. You can use empty soda fridge packs to store cans of soup; just cut a can-sized hole out of the top of the other end so that you can drop new purchases in easily. Cover your boxes with craft paper and label them nicely if you're crafty or want them to be pretty. Look around your home for storage materials to repurpose.

Also watch for sales at stores like Menards on sturdy shelving. (Here, look for wooden pressboard shelves rather than wire shelving, since cans and bottles don't stand well on the all-metal ones.) Build simple shelving with plywood and 2x4s in your basement, or add a high wooden shelf over the window in your laundry room. Again, it doesn't have to be fancy.

Instead of buying new, you can also stalk garage sales for creative storage solutions to repurpose. A basket in the bathroom can hold toiletries and tissue; a plastic tote in your laundry room can store bottles of detergent and fabric softener. Stockpile items don't have to be in your face and don't have to take over your home, as long as you keep them organized and contained.

Organize Small Spaces

If you're in a small apartment or home, get creative with your storage. Add bed risers and store items in shallow boxes underneath, add slim-line wall cabinets to hold cans, spices, and other small items.

TIPS AND TRICKS

Over-the-door shoe organizers aren't just for shoes! Add one to the inside of a pantry door to hold small items like seasoning packets or tuna pouches. You can also even add a plastic shoe organizer on the wall inside your shower to hold items like razors and shampoo.

You can also add wire racks or shelving to the insides of closet and cupboard doors to hold items like foil, plastic wrap, and sandwich bags. Add a rack under your sink to hold sponges and dish soap; add hooks to the insides of doors to hold items like spoons and measuring cups to clear out more drawer space for other items. You have many options for keeping items stored tidily out of sight.

Add a Freezer

If you have the room, you definitely want to invest in a second freezer. This lets you stock up on clearance sales on fresh meat and frozen veggies, freeze summer produce (like berries and peppers) when it's cheap at the store, and stock up on frozen veggies when sales on seasonal produce are scarce.

Chest freezers are more energy efficient but harder to keep organized, so decide if you're the type of person to let items languish in the depths. If you are particularly worried, attach a running list to the inside of the lid to help you keep track of what you have and what you're using. You can also use plastic bins to corral "like" items inside your chest freezer; this both helps keep it organized and helps you find items more quickly.

Some grocery stores run freezer promotions during Frozen Food Month in March, selling chest freezers at a discount and throwing in hundreds of dollars' worth of coupons for free items. Keep your eye out for these.

Weeding and Donating

Couponing and stockpiling work together, giving you the tools you need to reach out to others. You will sometimes find you have excess products that you've gotten very cheaply or free. You will sometimes find that you can pick up items for free that your family has no need of. You will sometimes find that, when you rotate or clean out your stockpile, you have items close to their expiration dates that could use good homes.

And you can consciously choose to coupon for others. There's always someone else who can use the items you can't. This is part of the answer to the puzzle of having to buy multiple items to save more: earmark some for you, and some for others.

So let's talk about what to keep, what to weed out, what to donate, and how to organize your bounty.

What to Keep

When you buy new stockpile items, be sure to rotate your stock. Add newer items with further-out expiration dates to the back of the shelf, and move older items to the front so that you're sure to use them first.

Use a site like StillTasty (stilltasty.com) to see how long you can keep items on the shelf or in the fridge, and to get storage guidelines to help keep products fresh. Be careful about storing food items and OTC medication in a garage or anywhere that the temperature and humidity fluctuates.

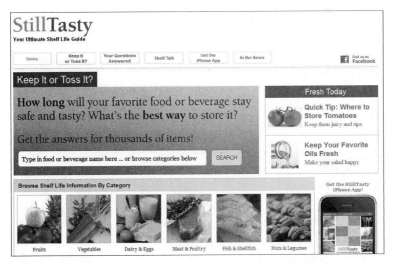

StillTasty gives guidelines for storing various food items.

When in doubt, do toss it—keep your family safe!—but check the guidelines first.

COUPON QUIPS

"Best by," "Best if used by," and "Use by" dates on packaged shelf-stable food items refer to a manufacturer's estimate of peak quality, rather than a date when the item instantly goes bad. This is not true of drugs or anything with an active ingredient, which start to lose potency after expiration.

Try to go through your stockpile every month or two. See where you have extra items, what you're not likely to use, and what's nearing expiration. Sometimes you'll find that your family doesn't care for a new brand, or that you overestimated how much you would use. Be truly willing to give up some items. Again, couponing shouldn't lead to hoarding, and there will always be another deal.

Where to Donate

We all know about local food banks, but there are many other organizations in need of our help, especially in these tough economic times.

Pick a cause that is near and dear to your heart, which will give you a personal incentive to reach out and help. Here are some ideas to get you started:

- Animal shelters—which can also use your extra newspapers to line cages.

- Domestic violence shelters.

- Food pantries—which usually take health and beauty items plus paper goods, not just food.

- Homeless shelters.

- Military organizations—VFWs and the USO may collect items to send care packages to the troops.

- Mission trips.

- The Salvation Army.

- Senior citizen homes and centers.

- Veterans' organizations.

- Your local house of worship.

Talk to each organization to see which items they're most in need of, then keep an eye out for these when weeding or shopping.

Also talk to your accountant or tax advisor when it comes to claiming these donations at tax time. Many take the stance that you can claim the value before coupons of donated items, but you'll want to check to see what your own advisor recommends.

You can also donate directly to friends and relatives who have fallen on hard times. It's much easier to accept a bag of groceries than financial assistance, especially if you stress that you were cleaning out your pantry and "know how the kids love brownies," or say something like "you know how I coupon, well, I went a little overboard so thought you might be able to take some off my hands."

Donating Seasonally

Some couponers gather items for donation across the year or on seasonal markdowns and donate them for specific drives or events. Organizations that fill backpacks with school supplies would love the free pens and pencils and filler paper you pick up each summer, and organizations that fill holiday boxes for kids would love everything from toiletries to toys. If you collect across the year for a specific cause, you can really see that you're making an impact as items pile up.

See if your place of worship or a local organization sponsors holiday boxes, mitten trees, or back-to-school backpack drives. Pick up items starting as soon as the post-holiday sales in January, or the back-to-school clearance sales in September.

You can also pick up 75 percent off toys at the semi-annual Target and Kmart toy clearances (around mid-January and again in mid-July) and save them for organizations like Toys for Tots or the adopt-a-family trees at the end of the year.

Donating for Disaster Relief

We've recently seen some horrific natural disasters that have hit close to home, and couponing offers us one way to reach out and help those in the affected areas. Some of the items we most commonly stockpile or can pick up for free after coupons, such as deodorant, toothpaste, body wash, shelf-stable food, and over-the-counter medications, are some of the items most needed for distribution in affected areas.

> **TIPS AND TRICKS**
>
> Talk to your local stores about adding a donation bin for disaster relief, or see if local churches or other organizations are organizing drives. It's more effective to centralize donations if possible.

Local bloggers near affected areas often organize drives and tours. Hip 2 Save, for instance, organized a Hip2Help tour after the April 2011 tornados and floods that devastated the American southeast, while Couponing to Disney organized disaster donation drives to help relief efforts in Alabama and Missouri. Readers could send in requested stockpile or purchased items to one central location, and these bloggers ensured that the items reached their intended recipients.

Also be sure to stockpile for emergencies in your own area. If you're stocked up on items like bottled water, shelf-stable ready-to-eat food items, and batteries, you'll be better prepared for anything that hits.

Couponing to Donate

Beyond regularly donating items that you've stockpiled but your family hasn't consumed, you can also think about couponing specifically to purchase donation items. We've talked all along about how high-value coupons, combined with sales or money-back offers, can often get us items for pennies on the dollar or for free. When your family can't use these, you can instead buy them for others.

Using coupons to purchase items to donate allows us to give much more than we otherwise could. Stretch your donation dollars by picking up items for free or for pennies on the dollar and turning right around and giving them to others. You can swing right by your local food pantry after a trip to the grocery store and unload your trunk; you can fill seasonal or disaster relief donation bins without even leaving the store.

Some of the items we can always get for free are sought-after donation items. Toothpaste, for one, is free so very often after coupons and cash back at the drugstores that I'd have to build a separate room to hold it all if I took full advantage of every offer. And guess what? The active ingredient expires! Instead of hoarding items my family will never use, I simply keep a year's supply under my sink (you never know ...), but buy more to donate whenever it's free.

Donating Expired Coupons

Families at overseas military bases are able to use manufacturer coupons at their commissary up to six months expired. You'll find that you never use all the coupons you acquire, and donating them to military families ensures that they don't go to waste.

Due to shipping and distribution times, most programs recommend that you don't send coupons more than two months expired at the time of shipment. They do appreciate clipped coupons rather than entire inserts, sorted into food and nonfood envelopes or baggies. This saves time on the other end, and saves you postage.

TIPS AND TRICKS

If you participate in a local coupon swap, ask members to bring in their clipped and sorted expired coupons so that you can put together a single box to ship.

At OCP (Overseas Coupon Program; ocpnet.org), you can adopt a base and send your coupons directly there. Since bases are U.S. territories, you don't have to pay overseas postage. The easiest way to ship coupons is to pick up a flat-rate priority-mail box at the post office, stuff it full, and send it off.

If you'd rather send these directly to an individual family rather than a base, Coupons to Troops (couponstotroops.com) gives suggestions on finding an overseas family to send coupons to. Lastly, you can send expired coupons to Coups for Troops (www.coupsfortroops. com), who will sort and mail them directly to individual families at various overseas bases.

If you have some coupons that haven't quite expired that you're not planning on using, you can also leave them by their matching items at the store for others to pick up and use. Do a good deed by leaving your diapers coupons right by the Pampers and your cat food coupons right by the Purina. Maybe you'll get someone else started on the path to saving.

Sharing and Trading

Back in Chapter 14, we talked about coupon swaps. You can also think about trading stockpile items with other local couponers. You might be swimming in cereal, but running low on peanut butter, while your neighbor instead went overboard on the last Skippy deal but is out of cornflakes.

Keep an ear out and listen to what your friends and family need. If your mother-in-law is complaining about the rising price of coffee, bring a couple of bags to your next family gathering. If your teenage nephews are eating your sister out of house and home, be the cool aunt who always shows up with bags of snacks. If your friend's kid is obsessed with Goldfish crackers, bring some along to your next playdate. Take advantage of every opportunity to share with others.

The Least You Need to Know

- Keep things organized so nothing gets lost or goes to waste.
- If you can't use it, someone else can: coupon to donate, and give freely from your stockpile.
- Trade and share with others; your stockpile is there to be used.

The Future of Couponing

In This Chapter

- Rising restrictions on coupon use
- Increasing restrictions on acquiring coupons
- The move toward nonpaper coupons
- Personalized deals and what that means to you

The couponing landscape is changing for many reasons, including: recent high-profile couponing shows that have made both stores and manufacturers nervous, the dramatic rise in coupon usage, new electronic and mobile technologies, and the ongoing push by manufacturers to control the ways in which their coupons are redeemed.

This chapter takes a look at these recent changes and how they affect couponers. It outlines new restrictions and potential future changes you should be aware of—but, throughout, shows how we can modify our strategies and still continue to plan to save big.

Restrictions

The rising popularity of couponing has made manufacturers more aware of, and concerned about, the ways in which their coupons are being redeemed. (We talked about this a bit back in the section on ethical couponing in Chapter 4.) This in turn has prompted new controls over the way coupons are used, distributed, and redeemed at the register—which will affect the way in which you plan out your trips.

Here are some recent changes and ideas on ways to adapt.

Per Transaction Wording

Some companies and stores are now limiting the number of "like" coupons you can use in a single transaction, or shopping order. This means that you can use only a specified number of the same coupon. If the "like" coupon limit is four, but you want to buy five items and use five coupons, you'll have to split your trip into two separate transactions—or in some cases, across two separate days.

These new restrictions stem from concerns about couponers who pick up cartsful of identical items at a time. Some companies and stores are also worried that shoppers may be reselling items at other stores or at flea markets, rather than purchasing them for personal use.

Major corporations, such as Procter & Gamble, have begun adding "limit of four like coupons in same shopping trip" wording onto the manufacturer coupons they distribute through Sunday newspaper inserts. Other companies have gone so far as to even state "one coupon per transaction" on some of their manufacturer coupons.

COUPON QUIPS

Know the difference between a transaction, which refers to your entire shopping trip, and a purchase, which refers to the qualifying item(s) purchased.

Most manufacturer coupons state something like "one per purchase," which simply means you can use one on each qualifying item or set of items you're purchasing. (Purchasing four packs of Pampers? Use four $1.00/1 coupons.) A transaction refers to your entire shopping order, so "one per shopping trip" or "one per transaction" applies to everything you are purchasing at one time.

Currently, these types of manufacturer-imposed like-coupon limits depend on cashiers reading the wording on coupons. Even if the coupon states "limit of four like coupons," that fifth like coupon won't beep at the register. New barcode formats, however, may change this in the near future.

Like coupon limits can frustrate shoppers when stores require the purchase of multiple items to receive a discount. If you have to buy five like items to receive a $5 instant in-store savings, a four-coupon limit can be frustrating. One approach here is to look elsewhere for different coupons to use for your like items. If you have three coupons from your local paper, and two printed coupons with different redemption values and expiration dates, these are not like coupons—even if they're for the same product.

Changing Coupon Policies

As with manufacturers, stores are nervous about some of the recent portrayals of out-of-control couponing behavior, and frustrated by some couponers who clear entire shelves of loss leaders and leave little or no products behind for others.

This has led to new store coupon policies, including the following:

- June 2011: Target bans printables for free items and disallows a buy-one-get-one coupon (BOGO) on a buy-one-get-one sale.

- April 2011: Kroger in Houston ends double and triple coupons.

- July 2011: Albertsons in the Pacific Northwest no longer has "twice the value" coupons in store, only in Sunday newspapers.

- June 2011: Shaw's in the Northeast limits like doubled coupons to four; customers can't split transactions to avoid this rule.

- May 2011: Rite Aid limits customers to four of one like coupon per transaction and prohibits BOGO coupons on BOGO sales.

It's likely that we'll see these types of changes continuing and spreading across more grocery store and drugstore chains as stores update their corporate coupon policies.

HEADS-UP

Watch for coupon policy changes from your stores, as stores are updating policies more often than in the past in response to pressure from manufacturers and other shoppers. These changes are often announced on local blogs or posted on signs in the store. You don't want surprises at the register to mess up your careful coupon plan!

Some stores, such as Target, don't specify an official number limit of like items or coupons—but do reserve the right to limit purchases to "normal family quantities." What this means is completely up to the store and cashier, so is fairly arbitrary. (And a family of four will have completely different shopping and stock-up patterns than a family of eight!) Walgreens specifically reserves the right to limit quantities, and many Walgreens stores in heavy couponing areas have begun limiting shoppers to one like Register Rewards or in-ad coupon deal per day.

As stores change their coupon policies, couponers need to adapt their shopping strategies. You might move some of your shopping to stores with more lenient coupon policies; you might start subscribing to the Sunday paper rather than relying on picking up doubler coupons in store; you might make a couple of trips during the week (or bring your significant other along to do a separate transaction!) if you want to pick up multiple items.

In the end, though, limits can sometimes work in couponers' favor. It's frustrating to head to your local store for a great deal, only to find an empty shelf. When stores impose limits, more shoppers are able to get in on the sales, even if we're not able to purchase higher quantities of products.

Remember also that items tend to hit their lowest price at the store once about every three months. While it's good to stock up on a quantity that your family will use, you don't need to invest in a year's supply of most items—there will always be another deal. So store limits can also help you think about how many items your family actually needs.

Particularly when we're new to couponing, it's easy to want to get in on every deal and to pick up as many products as possible. It's just not necessary though: There will always be another rock bottom sale on deodorant and body wash and toothpaste at the drugstore. There will always be another loss leader cereal or granola bar sale at the grocery store.

Crackdowns on Clippers

Manufacturers aren't particularly fond of clipping services or coupon clippers on eBay. Clippers allow couponers to easily purchase multiples of high-value coupons.

When manufacturers release a high-value coupon, their goals are to raise brand awareness and create repeat customers. They're not deliberately looking to let you walk out of the store with multiple items for free or for pennies on the dollar, and their target consumer is not the customer who bops between brands and buys multiple items at rock-bottom prices using coupons.

Online sales of coupons can also result in a much higher than predicted rate of redemption for a coupon, as customers purchase multiple copies in preparation for a hot sale at their local store. Manufacturers might expect 4 percent of the coupons they issue to be redeemed in a given area, but when people buy multiples from clippers, that number might double. When companies haven't budgeted for that increase, they're thrown into a tizzy.

Manufacturers point to the "void if transferred or sold" wording on most manufacturers coupons as invalidating these types of sales. Clippers and eBay sellers claim they're charging for their time to clip the coupons, rather than the coupons themselves.

HEADS-UP

In February 2011, the industry group Coupon Information Corporation (CIC) began sending certified letters to a number of coupon sellers on eBay, asking them to stop all eBay sales and sign a memorandum of understanding stating that they'd done so. (How'd they get the seller's address? They bought coupons from them!) This was not a legal challenge, however, just a threatening request—and most eBay sellers ignored the letter and continued on their merry way.

For now, business is proceeding largely as usual, but this again is worth keeping an eye on. The industry might well put more pressure on clippers in the future.

If you rely on picking up clipped coupons because you're in an area that no longer sees Sunday newspaper inserts, or are in a rural area with limited coupons and lower values, you will want to start looking at alternatives now. Look into swapping coupons with friends, coupon swaps at libraries, trading boards, private sellers, and coupon trains to acquire your coupons without having to rely on eBay or the various services. (See more on acquiring additional coupons in Chapter 14.) Also be sure to print coupons at the beginning of each month when the major sites release a new big batch.

Limits on Newspaper Purchases

Stores that sell the Sunday newspaper at a discount, such as The Dollar Tree, Menards, and Deals, have in many areas begun limiting the number of Sunday papers each customer may purchase, usually to three. On a high-value coupon week, you might well want more than three, so your alternatives are to invest in multiple subscriptions, visit multiple stores, or bring along a spouse, child, or friend to pick up your other papers.

Look online for coupon codes to get your Sunday newspaper subscriptions at a discount; these are often available on local coupon blogs or on sites like RetailMeNot.com. Discount subscriptions also sometimes pop up on daily deals sites like Groupon, which has, for example, offered the Sunday *Chicago Tribune* for $.25 a week (as opposed to $1.00 a week).

New Barcodes

This particular change has been in the works for years. New GS1 barcodes on coupons can carry much more information, preventing people from using coupons on products they're not intended for. This is unquestionably a good thing, since using barcode decoding to pick up free products by using coupons that are intended for other products is, plainly, stealing.

However these new barcodes can also contain other information, this includes start date. So if you pick up an early edition of a Sunday paper on Saturday, you might not be able to use the coupons on Saturday if they don't activate until Sunday. GS1 barcodes can also specify a geographical region. So if you buy a paper while on vacation in another state and bring home the coupons to use at your local store, they may beep at the register. This may also eventually put an end to printing coupons online that are released in other ZIP codes.

We'll have to watch and see what happens as the new barcodes and registers to read them are phased in. As of now, these specific restrictions aren't a reality, but it's good to be aware of what might be coming down the pike.

Nonpaper

We've already talked about the fact that both stores and manufacturers like the idea of electronic and mobile coupons. We can expect the use of these to expand in the future, as manufacturers enjoy the control this gives them, the information they can collect about you, and the ability to personalize offers to each consumer. Stores see faster checkout lines if cashiers don't need to scan coupons, and the ability to target coupons toward specific individuals or demographics.

So what does the move toward electronic coupons mean to us as couponers? In part, these mean more limits. Since these are tied to your card or a mobile app, you can't just go and clip more coupons.

Luckily, though, these changes are slow in coming. Some stores and companies are finding that the move to electronic coupons isn't as smooth as anticipated. Electronic-only coupons also disadvantage people who are less comfortable with computers or who lack home Internet access, so there has been some push-back from that end. Right now we see both paper coupons and electronic coupons in widespread use. Take advantage of this, because the more ways we have to save, the better.

Personalization

Stores and manufacturers are taking a good hard look at personalizing the couponing experience. Stores are trying to personalize the deals available to their shoppers by offering them electronic coupons and personalized discounts on specific items they might be interested in. So even if your friend or relative has a specific e-coupon or personalized offer on her card, you might not have the same option available to you. Sometimes this works out well for consumers, and sometimes it backfires.

The Safeway Experiment

Safeway is an interesting experiment, because in addition to the "Coupon Center" that contains electronic coupons, its Just for U also offers a "Personalized Deals" section. Personalized deals are not coupons. Instead, they offer a personalized price on a product that is lower than the store's everyday price. If you load a personalized price to your card, you'll receive either that price or the current sale price, whichever is lower.

HEADS-UP

Personalized deals are attached to an individual's loyalty card, so the personalized deals I receive will not be the same as the personalized deals you receive. This makes it hard to share info and can be frustrating when others talk about great deals that aren't available to you.

How does Safeway decide what personalized deals to offer? These are billed as "Great deals on items you buy, and items we think you will like"—which are sometimes savings on items you have bought, but are often on competing brands to the one you usually buy, or brands of complete randomness. (I often have personalized prices for dog food on my own Just for U—but I've never owned a dog!)

What's the best thing about personalized pricing? We talked way back at the beginning of this journey about knowing when a deal is really a deal. Sometimes a deal isn't a deal because stores tend to price the first item very, very high on a buy-one-get-one free

(BOGO) sale. Well, what happens when you have a lower personalized price on an item than the store is offering on its BOGO sale?

You guessed it! Since your personalized price supersedes the store's high price on the sale, you'll get your buy-one-get-one free deal at that low personalized price. So let's say that your store is offering Jennie-O ground turkey BOGO at $5.99. But you have a personalized deal offer for Jennie-O ground turkey at $2.48. That's right: you, and only you, get your ground turkey BOGO at $2.48—so you can now buy two for $2.48, rather than two for $5.99.

> **TIPS AND TRICKS**
>
> The same personalized pricing bonus tends to apply to instant savings deals, such as when you instantly save $4 when you buy four participating items. When your items ring up at a lower personalized price, that instant savings then comes off that lower price rather than the normal high before instant-savings price.

So if your store offers any kind of personalized electronic savings, be sure to check their e-coupon site whenever they're running a buy-one-get-one free or instant savings sale to see if you have a low personalized price for that item.

SuperValu

Beyond the personalized prices found on Safeway's Just for U, other stores are personalizing the actual electronic coupons on their sites. On SuperValu's Avenu e-coupon sites, the electronic coupons available vary by card, both in terms of specific products and in value. This is again supposed to be linked to products you've bought in the past.

Meijer

While the printable store coupons on Meijer's Mealbox site (www.meijermealbox.com) are the same for every visitor, mPerks mobile coupons (www.meijer.com/mperks) can vary. Meijer, for instance, randomly texts alerts for $2 off a $2 purchase and $5 off a $5 purchase. Some people receive $2, some people receive $5, and some people receive nothing—and Meijer's not sharing the magic formula by which they determine who receives what.

Don't Lose Hope

With all of these new restrictions and changes, it's easy to become frustrated and feel that you got into couponing at just the wrong time. Trust me: there is no wrong time to start couponing. Talk to any couponer from any era, and you'll hear stories about the good old days. Store policies have always evolved, and new restrictions always arise. We always continue to do well, and there's always another deal to be had.

Stores like Walmart are actually bucking the trend and changing their policies to be much more friendly to couponers than ever before. Their policy to allow cash back when you have a coupon worth more than the price of an item, for instance, is both huge and unprecedented, and you can bet that other stores will be watching a giant like Walmart to learn from their experiences. Some of these tighter policies could well be a temporary backlash, and we never know how things will change when the excitement dies down.

New ways of coupon savings, like electronic coupons, SMS coupons, and apps, also offer opportunities we never had in the past. The ability to save online and at retail stores through cash-back programs, coupon codes, apps, and more allows us to remain afloat in an era of ever increasing prices.

Our ability to share information online is also invaluable. Instead of my telling one or two friends about a great deal at our local grocery store, I can now broadcast it to the world on a blog, Facebook, online forum, Twitter, or wherever people want to receive that information. The more pairs of eyes we have looking out for the deals, the better.

The Least You Need to Know

- New restrictions are changing our couponing strategies.
- Expect manufacturers and stores to continue slowly but surely moving away from paper coupons.
- Coupon personalization offers both new opportunities and new challenges.

Glossary

AY An abbreviation for *All You* magazine. Found only at Walmart or by subscription, this magazine always contains a number of manufacturer coupons.

B&M (or BM) Stands for "Brick and Mortar," or physical, as opposed to online, stores.

big box stores Large retailers that feature big stores and everyday low prices.

blinkies Coupons that are found in machines attached directly to store shelves. These machines have blinking lights on them to attract customers' attention.

BOGO Stands for buy-one-get-one free.

Catalina A coupon for a specific item or a dollar amount off your next shopping trip that prints out of machines by the register when you purchase specific qualifying items.

cherry picking Shopping at multiple stores in a given week to snag just the top deals from each.

coupon train A group of people who join together to swap coupons. The first member mails an envelope full of coupons to the second member. She pulls out the ones she wants, replaces with an equal number of coupons, and sends to the next member on the train. It keeps going infinitely!

CRT Cash Register Tape, is used as shorthand for coupons that print out right on your receipt at the store.

e-coupon Electronic coupon. You load these coupons directly onto your grocery store loyalty card. The discount automatically comes off at the register when you purchase the appropriate product.

endcap Displays of products at the end of an aisle.

ExtraCare Bucks (ECB) At CVS, store coupons for dollars off your next shopping order, are called Extra (Care) Bucks.

FAQ Frequently Asked Questions. A list of common questions and answers found on websites, including couponing sites.

filler At Walgreens, a filler is a small low-cost item for your Register Rewards to "attach" to if you want to use multiple coupons per transaction. It can also be a low-cost item you throw into your shopping trip in order to get up to a specific dollar amount so you can use a Catalina to pay for your purchases.

FSI Free Standing Insert. Refers to the multiple-coupon inserts found in the Sunday newspaper.

hangtags Coupons that hang from the neck of a product in the store.

HBA Health and Beauty Aisle. HBA items include everything from toiletries to over-the-counter medication.

like coupon Aka, identical coupon. Some stores limit the number of "like," or identical, coupons you can use per transaction.

loss leader A product that the store puts on super-sale, often selling it at a loss to attract customers who will also spend a lot of money on additional higher-priced items.

matchup A list of store sales and their corresponding coupons.

MIR Mail In Rebate.

mfr. An abbreviation for manufacturer, as in *mfr. coupon.*

OTC "Over the counter." OTC medication can be bought off the shelf without a prescription.

out-of-pocket (OOP) The actual amount of cash money you spend on your shopping trips after coupons and discounts is your out-of-pocket cost.

overage   When you have a coupon whose value is more than the price of the item, that creates overage—which in some cases you can apply toward other items in your order.

OYNO (or OYNSO)   Stands for: On Your Next Order or On Your Next Shopping Order. OYNO Catalinas are coupons that you can use to save a certain dollar amount off your next shopping trip.

peelies   Coupon stickers that are attached directly to a product; customers peel the coupon off and use it at the store.

PG (P&G)   Procter & Gamble's monthly coupon insert.

price book   Consumers used to keep a notebook with a list of the prices each week on their favorite items to get a sense of how prices fluctuated over time and when a sale was really a good deal.

purchase   An item in your shopping order. Coupons that state "one per purchase" mean one coupon can be used per item.

Q   Online shorthand for coupon.

QR codes   Quick Response codes. These special barcodes can store information such as web addresses. When a mobile phone user scans a QR code in store, in an ad, in a magazine, or on a product with a QR scanner app, the information contained in that code is automatically delivered to their phone.

rain checks   Available at customer service when a store is out of stock on a sale item; allows you to pick up that item for that same sale price at a later date.

RAOK   Random Act of Kindness. Couponers are a sharing group, and often give other couponers high-value coupons they themselves are unable to use.

Register Rewards (RR)   Catalina coupons that print out at Walgreens for dollars off your next shopping order; Walgreens' Catalina program.

rolling   When you use a Catalina coupon to purchase new Catalina-producing items, you minimize your own out-of-pocket cost and can continue using your play money in this way indefinitely.

RP   Stands for the RedPlum coupon insert.

RSS   Real Simple Syndication. Allows readers to subscribe to blogs and other online content, all in one place.

SCR   Single Check Rebate at Rite Aid. Enter receipts for qualifying rebate items online, and request one check for all your rebates at the end of the month.

SS   SmartSource coupon insert.

stacking   When you add together multiple ways of saving on a single item; for example, using a paper coupon with an electronic coupon and a sale price.

stockpile   A collection of products couponers purchase for pennies on the dollar and then live off of instead of paying full price for necessary items as you run out of them.

thread   All the responses to a single topic on an online forum.

TIA   Thanks In Advance. When couponers ask for help and advice on forums and blogs, they might sign off with this as a preemptive thank you.

TMF   Stands for "try me free." A rebate that gives back the full purchase price of an item.

transaction   All the items you are purchasing in a single shopping trip or payment. If you ring groups of items up separately, and pay for each group separately, each of those groups comprises a separate transaction.

tweet   A comment on Twitter.

unmoderated forum   An online community in which anyone can post anything.

+UP Rewards   At Rite Aid, these coupons for dollars off your next shopping order print out when you purchase qualifying items.

WYB   When You Buy.

YMMV   Your Mileage May Vary, meaning that a deal might not work out the same way for everyone.

YourBucks   *See* Catalina.

Online Resources

Use online resources to maximize your coupon savings, both at the store and online. Here are some ideas to get you started. You'll also want to search out local bloggers in your own area as well as resources for your own diet and needs.

Coupon Blogs

Coupon blogs are a great resource for everything from matchups for local stores to keeping you aware of new online deals.

Common Sense with Money—www.commonsensewithmoney.com
She partners with bloggers nationwide to provide matchups for over 100 grocery stores.

Couponing to Disney—www.couponingtodisney.com
One of the largest couponing blogs; offers "five a day" lists of manufacturers to write to for coupons and more.

Coupons, Deals and More—couponsdealsandmore.com
Highlights here include weekly previews of upcoming newspaper insert coupons.

Deal Seeking Mom—dealseekingmom.com
Covers matchups for over 50 stores on her "Grocery Grab" and more.

For the Mommas—forthemommas.com
Everything from drugstore deals to coupon codes to printable coupons and more.

The Frugal Map—thefrugalmap.bargainbriana.com/the-frugal-map
Start here to find coupon bloggers in your local area.

The Grocery Gathering—www.becentsable.net/store-deals
Another listing of coupon bloggers by state.

Hip 2 Save—hip2save.com
One of the biggest and highest-trafficked coupon blogs.

i heart cvs—www.iheartcvs.com
Specializes in CVS matchups and deals; also preview future ads.

I Heart the Mart—www.iheartthemart.com
Walmart matchups and deals, although note that prices vary
regionally.

i heart wags—www.iheartwags.com
Focuses on Walgreens matchups and deals; also preview future ads.

Jill Cataldo—jillcataldo.com
Both a coupon blog and a forum; she also spotlights new develop-
ments in the industry.

Mashup Mom—mashupmom.com
Your author's site, covering both store coupon matchups and online
deals.

Meijer Madness—meijermadness.com
Focuses on Meijer deals.

Mojo Savings—mojosavings.com
Find freebies, deals, and more.

Money Saving Madness—www.moneysavingmadness.com
Drugstore matchups, retail and restaurant coupons, online deals, and
more.

Money Saving Mom—moneysavingmom.com
One of the oldest blogs in the genre; she also talks about budgeting
and provides frugality advice.

My Frugal Adventures—myfrugaladventures.com
Find matchups for Publix, Kroger, Harris Teeter, drugstores, and
more.

Printable Coupons and Deals—printablecouponsanddeals.net
Lots and lots of printable coupons—and deals!

Totally Target—www.totallytarget.com
Focuses on Target matchups and deals, plus lists which Target print-able coupons are manufacturer, which are store, and how to stack.

Wild for Wags—wildforwags.com
Focuses on Walgreens deals.

Coupon Databases

Use these to look up which newspaper insert contained a particular coupon and where else coupons for a given product might be found.

Coupon Tom—coupontom.com
Look up coupons and see what insert they were in. Create an account and you can also search expired coupons back a specified number of days.

Hot Coupon World—www.hotcouponworld.com/forums/coupon. php
Includes coupons from all sources: Inserts, brochures, blinkies, tearpads, mailers, and more.

Coupon Forums

Join in the discussions here as people across the country share info on coupons and deals.

FatWallet—www.fatwallet.com
Pick the forums tab to join in the discussions—especially good for online deals.

A Full Cup—afullcup.com
Many of their sub-forums contain weekly matchups and discussions for various stores.

Hot Coupon World—www.hotcouponworld.com/forums
One of the biggest forums out there, covers just about any coupon-ing topic.

Slickdeals—slickdeals.net
Very good for online deals and codes as well as information on Catalina deals.

WeUseCoupons—www.weusecoupons.com
In addition to discussion forums, check out their YouTube channel for couponing videos and view hot forum highlights right on the front page.

Coupon-Printing Sites

Print manufacturer coupons right from your own computer for extra savings at the store.

Coupon Network—www.couponnetwork.com
Owned by the Catalina corporation; often offers different coupons than on the other sites.

Coupons.com—www.coupons.com
The biggest coupon-printing site, often containing 150–200 coupons.

RedPlum—www.redplum.com
The smallest national coupon-printing site, but sometimes contains unique or limited-time special coupons.

SmartSource—smartsource.com
Run by the people who produce the Sunday insert of the same name.

Target—coupons.target.com
Find both Target store coupons and manufacturer printables here.

Online Shopping

Combine coupon codes with sales with cash-back offers for the best deals.

Cash-Back Rebate Sites

Cash-back sites give you a percentage of the purchase price back when you click through them to do your online shopping.

Ebates—www.ebates.com
In addition to cash back at hundreds of online retailers, they run "daily doubles" and other bonus cash-back specials.

ebillMe—www.ebillme.com
They offer cash back on gift cards, but you have to check out with eBillMe and pay through your online banking.

FatWallet—www.fatwallet.com
More than a forum; offers cash back from many online retailers.

Mr. Rebates—mrrebates.com
Check here for cash-back offers for hundreds of retailers.

SavingStar—savingstar.com
Get cash back when you load offers as "e-coupons" onto your grocery and drugstore loyalty cards.

Upromise—www.upromise.com
Get cash back into college savings.

Comparison Shopping Sites

Compare prices here to ensure you're getting the best deal.

NexTag—www.nextag.com
Enter the name of a product and your ZIP code and see the price including shipping and tax at various stores.

PriceGrabber—www.pricegrabber.com
See a product's final price at various online retailers.

Coupon Code Sites

Find coupon codes to save on all your online purchases.

CouponCabin—www.couponcabin.com
Put in the name of an online retailer and find current coupon codes.

FreeShipping.org—www.freeshipping.org
Focuses entirely on free shipping codes; some of which require a minimum purchase or are only for certain product categories.

RetailMeNot—www.retailmenot.com
The biggest coupon code database, also includes user-submitted codes.

Deals-of-the-Day Sites

Each of these contains different limited-time deals each day.

1SaleADay—1saleaday.com
Deeply discounted products—many are refurbs or older, though.

Amazon Gold Box—www.amazon.com/gp/goldbox
Daily deals plus "lightning" deals that change over every couple hours or so.

BuyWithMe—www.buywithme.com
Buy a deal, share it with friends, and if three of them also buy yours is free.

CityPockets—www.citypockets.com
Keep track of all your daily deals in one place, and buy and resell deal vouchers.

CoupRecoup—couprecoup.com
Buy and sell daily deal vouchers—they call themselves the "Craigslist for Groupon."

DealsGoRound—www.dealsgoround.com
Buy vouchers from others, sell your own, and organize your daily deal vouchers.

Eversave—www.eversave.com
Many online deals plus some local.

FamilyFinds—www.familyfinds.com
Focuses on family-friendly deals, both online and local.

Groupon—www.groupon.com
The one that started it all; many cities feature multiple daily deals.

LivingSocial—livingsocial.com
Buy a deal, share it with friends, if three buy, yours is free. Like Groupon, generally offers multiple deals in larger markets.

MYHABIT—www.myhabit.com
Amazon's designer daily deals site.

Saveology—www.saveology.com
Offers online, offline, and gift card daily deals.

Target—dailydeals.target.com
Daily product deals on Target also ship free.

Tippr—tippr.com
More daily deals, often online.

Woot!—www.woot.com
One day, one deal; focuses on products and often features refurbs.

Organic, Natural, and Allergen-Free Couponing

The Frugal Seed—thefrugalseed.com
Helps readers save money while living naturally.

Gluten Free Birmingham—www.glutenfreebirmingham.com
Not all Birmingham, despite the name. Focuses on affordable gluten-free living.

Gluten-Free on a Shoestring—glutenfreeonashoestring.com
Tips for living gluten free on a tight budget; includes recipes, and more.

Gluten Freely Frugal—www.glutenfreelyfrugal.com
Coupons for gluten-free products, deals, recipes, and more.

Green Vegan Living—greenveganliving.blogspot.com
Green, gluten free, and Vegan—find recipes and more.

HealthESavers—healthesavers.com/HealthESavers/Coupons.aspx
Print coupons for natural and organic items.

Healthy Life Deals—www.healthylifedeals.com
Coupons, freebies, and deals for "a whole foods healthy life."

Mambo Sprouts—www.mambosprouts.com
Print coupons for organic, natural, green, and allergen-free products.

Mashup Mom Crunchy Friday—mashupmom.com/?cat=2892
Each Friday I sum up the week's best natural, organic, green, and allergen-free deals and coupons.

Organic Cents—organiccents.blogspot.com
Focuses on organic deals and coupons.

Organic Deals—www.organicdeals.com
Online and offline organic deals, coupons, and more.

Organic Valley—www.organicvalley.coop/coupons
Print coupons for Organic Valley products.

Real Food, Allergy Free—www.realfoodallergyfree.com
Simple allergen-free, budget-friendly recipes.

Recyclebank—www.recyclebank.com
Earn points and then redeem them for high-value coupons for organic and natural products.

Saving Naturally—savingnaturally.com
Coupons, deals, and more for natural products.

Seventh Generation—www.seventhgeneration.com/coupons
Print coupons for Seventh Generation products.

Stonyfield Farms—www.stonyfield.com/user/register
Print coupons for Stonyfield Farms products.

The Thrifty Mama—www.thethriftymama.com
Tips on shopping and eating naturally on a budget.

Vegan Coupons—www.facebook.com/vegancoupons
Vegan coupons.

Whole Foods—www.wholefoodsmarket.com/coupons
Print monthly Whole Foods store coupons online.

Index

C

X-Y-Z